Equipping For Ministry

Phase III

Positional Truth

Pocket Principles®
and Guided Discussions

For Students

Positional Truth, **Pocket Principles® and Guided Discussions, For Students**
Equipping For Ministry
Second Edition

For copyright information:
Worldwide Discipleship Association
(Attention: Margaret Garner)
P.O. Box 142437
Fayetteville, GA 30214 USA
E-mail: mgarner@disciplebuilding.org
Web Site: www.disciplebuilding.org

NOTE: In an effort to recognize that both men and women are co-heirs of God's grace, we have chosen to use alternating gender pronouns in this document. However, we do recognize and embrace gender-specific roles in Scripture.

Development Team:
Bob Dukes
Margaret Garner
Jack Larson

Writing Team:
Bob Dukes
Margaret Garner
Jack Larson
Jon Long (Primary Author)

Publishing Team:
Nila Duffitt
Buddy Eades
Margaret Garner
David Parfitt

Positional_Truth_S_01.31.2018

Design by Cristina van de Hoeve
doodlingdesigner.com

A Welcome from WDA's President
Worldwide Discipleship Association, Inc.

Hello Friend!

Let me congratulate you on your decision to learn more about ministering to others in the name of Jesus Christ. This decision is critical in your continued growth as a disciple.

Understanding a Christian's position before God is a key to having a successful disciple building ministry. These studies will help you and others understand how our standing (position) before God was affected by the death and resurrection of Jesus and what the relationship is between the law and grace. We in WDA want to help you grow as a disciple and become all you can be in Christ Jesus!

My prayer and confident belief is that "he who began a good work in you will carry it on to completion until the day of Christ Jesus" (Philippians 1:6) so that He is able "to present you before his glorious presence without fault and with great joy." (Jude 1:24) To Him be glory and praise!

May God richly bless you as you strive to grow in Him.

Bob Dukes
President, Worldwide Discipleship Association, Inc.
Fayetteville, GA 30214

Positional Truth
Table of Contents: Student

Positional Truth

One of American author and satirist Mark Twain's most loved stories is that of *The Prince and the Pauper*. In this humorous tale, the crown prince of England, Edward, and a young outcast beggar, Tom, exchanged clothes and, hence, identities. Those around them did not believe them when each claimed to be himself. Yet Edward, even when suffering the abuse and insults that were Tom's lot in life, always knew he was heir to the throne. And Tom, enjoying the luxury and attention of life in the palace, knew that, in truth, he was still the son of a despised and abusive thieving drunkard.

This story highlights the importance of identity and the compelling influence that our standing or position has on how we view ourselves and how others view us. There are important lessons for the Christian in this story. Many Christians do not have a good understanding of their identity—their position in Christ—and therefore do not live like children of the King.

The antidote for this malady is "positional truth" for positional truth describes our true identity. This Pocket Principle™ is the introduction to a series of studies about positional truth. The Christian can better understand the critical nature of positional truth by answering the following four key questions.

WHAT IS POSITIONAL TRUTH?

Positional truth has to do with the changes that occurred in our identity when we trusted Christ at salvation. These changes were immediate and absolute, and they affected our standing, our state, and our position before God. They are true of all Christians whether they understand, experience or perceive them or not. Because these changes take place in the spiritual realm, they must be accepted as truth(s) by faith.

The opposite of positional truth is experiential truth. It is also known as temporal or practical truth. As its name suggests, experiential truth is something that Christians have the opportunity to experience in their everyday living. Experiential truth is gradual rather than immediate, and is characterized by change and fluctuation. Rather than occurring at a point in time, it is an ongoing reality.

> Positional truth has to do with changes that occurred in our identity when we trusted Christ at salvation.

A number of illustrations have been offered to explain what is meant by positional truth, including that of a citizen, a soldier, and a spouse. Perhaps the most helpful illustration is the relationship between a child and his parent.

I (Jon) have been blessed with four children—three boys and a girl. Consider my oldest son, for example. The day he was born, he was as much my son as he will ever be. For better or worse, he has grown to be more like me over the years, imitating my mannerisms and figures of speech. Many people say he looks a lot like me. Our relationship has grown richer over the years, as we have shared more experiences and much time with one another. However, he is neither more nor less my son now than he was the day of his birth. And he will always be my son. Even if I wanted to disown him (I shudder at the thought), he would still be my son. He may one day disown me (I shudder yet more), but he will still be my son. He could move far away, change his name, change his appearance, and do anything else he might think of to sever ties, but he will always have my DNA.

> From the moment of salvation, a Christian is born into God's family and forever after bears the divine DNA imprint.

The same is true of the Christian. The day that a person places his faith in Jesus Christ as his Savior, he becomes as much a child of God as he will ever be. It is not as though some things are true of him at the time of salvation and other things become true when he has further experiences in the Christian life. Certainly he will grow and mature in his Christian walk but, from the moment of salvation, he is born into God's family and forever after bears the divine DNA imprint.

In his writings, the Apostle Paul distinguishes spiritual Christians from immature Christians. It is important to note that he is referring to their practices—their daily walk—rather than to their spiritual standing. Positionally, there is no such thing as a spiritual Christian or an immature Christian. We all have been given fullness in Christ (Colossians 2:10). Experientially, we live at different points along the spectrum and, sadly, many must be considered to be immature.

WHY IS POSITIONAL TRUTH IMPORTANT?

<u>Positional truth is the basis of our relationship with Christ.</u>

Positional truth is comprised primarily of the things that Christ accomplished on the cross, because it was His death on the cross that has made possible our standing before God. It was at the cross that He provided the way for hostility to be ended, condemnation to be removed, sins to be forgiven, righteousness to be granted, and new life to begin. We would not have a relationship with God if it were not for the actions represented by positional truth.

<u>Positional truth is the basis for living the Christian life.</u>

The implications of truth are seen in a changed life. If a person has truly understood and embraced the foundational or positional truths of the gospel, he will live differently.

Paul often develops "positional" ideas first and then exhorts his readers to live in specific ways ("experiential" ideas) in light of those truths. First he says, "This is true." Then he goes on to say, "This is what should be true or should become more true."

Consider the following examples:

> **Colossians 3:1-2**—*Since then, you have been raised with Christ* (positional truth), *set your hearts on things above…set your minds on things above* (experiential truth).

> **Colossians 3:12**—*Therefore, as God's chosen people, holy and dearly loved* (positional truth), *clothe yourselves with compassion, kindness, humility, gentleness, and patience* (experiential truth).

> **Ephesians 5:8**—*For you were once darkness, but now you are light in the Lord* (positional truth). *Live as children of light* (experiential truth).

On a larger scale, entire sections of Paul's letters can be identified as primarily positional or primarily experiential in nature. For example, Paul develops the doctrine of justification by faith and its implications in the first 11 chapters of Romans. Then, in chapter 12, he begins telling his readers how they should live. Romans 12:1 starts out "Therefore, I urge you brothers and sisters, in view of God's mercy..."

Basically Paul is saying, "based on everything I have explained to you so far, this is how you should live; this is how you should respond to these truths."

<u>Positional truth prevents a fall back into legalism.</u>

Legalism is a mindset that says a Christian must perform in certain ways to be accepted by God. By contrast, the doctrine of grace, which is a positional truth, insists that the Christian is always and only accepted by God based on Christ's work on the cross. The early Christians in Galatia gladly received this message, which freed them from the hopeless pursuit of righteousness by keeping the law. However, they soon forgot the positional truths they had once embraced and began to rely on old patterns of thinking. Paul warned the Galatians that they were in danger of falling back into legalism because they were making works the basis of their relationship with Christ instead of the positional truths they must accept by faith. "You foolish Galatians! Who has bewitched you?" stormed Paul. His strong rebuke to these Christians highlights the importance that Paul (under the inspiration of the Holy Spirit) places on positional truth.

It is easy to fall into this subtle trap of the evil one. I (Jon) remember when, as a teenager, I would do things that I knew were displeasing to my parents and displeasing to God. I got into the habit of waiting to ask for forgiveness until some time had passed and I had the opportunity to prove myself (doing homework, helping out around the house, and so on). While this may seem like reasonable behavior from a human perspective, it represents a poor understanding of the truths of the gospel and is an insult to God, making Him out to be a liar by denying what He has said to be true.

<u>Positional truth helps us to overcome sin in our lives.</u>

> The doctrine of grace, a positional truth, insists that the Christian is always and only accepted by God based on Christ's work on the cross.

While understanding positional truth can prevent a fall back into legalism, it does not lead to license or the inappropriate use of our freedom. Far from it. After expounding the doctrines of grace, Paul asked rhetorically, "What shall we say, then? Shall we go on sinning so that grace may increase? By no means!" is Paul's response to his own question (Romans 6:1-2). A deep understanding of positional truth actually leads us to holiness. Paul based his exhortations to holy living on positional truth. Returning to Romans 12:1-2, we see that Paul considered the natural response to positional truth to be the offering of ourselves as "living sacrifices," holy and pleasing to God.

HOW CAN I RECOGNIZE POSITIONAL TRUTH?

There are two easy ways to identify positional truth in Scripture. The first is to observe changes in status (often stated as strong contrasts), and the second is to look for specific verbal clues.

Positional truth is truth that occurs at salvation and involves a permanent change of legal status with God. We had one standing before God prior to our salvation, and we have an entirely new and different standing before God after salvation. We have passed from death unto life; we have gone from darkness to light; we have transferred from Satan's kingdom to God's Kingdom; we have moved from slavery to freedom; we are no longer enemies but friends, no longer illegitimate children but sons and heirs of God. Consider Jesus' words recorded in John 5:24

as one example of this change in status: "Very truly I tell you the truth, whoever hears my word and believes Him who sent Me has eternal life and will not be judged but has crossed over from death to life." In these words of Jesus, notice not only the permanence ("eternal") but also the clear statement of a transition from one position to another.

As can be seen in several of the verses quoted above, there are verbal clues that often point us to positional truth. When we come across words like "because," "since," and "therefore," we can often determine that positional truth has just been explained.

There are also specific phrases that provide verbal clues. Examples of these include the following.

- At times, Paul uses the phrase "in Christ" to indicate that he is signaling a positional truth. For example, Paul wrote, "In the same way, count yourselves dead to sin but alive to God in Christ Jesus." (Romans 6:11) In Romans 16:7, Andronicus and Junias are described as being in Christ. This idea of being "in Christ" means that the Christian has been placed into Christ in such a way that what is true of Christ is true of the Christian. Christ is righteous; I am "in Christ"; therefore, I am righteous. Christ died; I am "in Christ"; therefore, I died. And so on.

- The phrase "baptism into Christ Jesus" also points to positional truth. In Romans 6:3-4, Paul writes, "Or don't you know that all of us who were baptized into Christ Jesus were baptized into His death? We were therefore buried with Him through baptism into death in order that, just as Christ was raised from the dead through the glory of the Father, we too may live a new life."

- "Union with Christ" is another term Paul used to point to positional truth. Romans 6:5 states that, "For if we have been united with Him in a death like His, we will certainly also be united with Him in a resurrection like His."

- In his letter to the Ephesians, Paul uses another term to emphasize position, that of being "seated with Christ." He writes in Ephesians 2:6, "And God raised us up with Christ and seated us with Him in the heavenly realms in Christ Jesus."

This idea of being in Christ or united with Christ is doubtless something of a mystery. We should always desire to understand these concepts better, but we need to be wary of trying so hard to plumb the depths of the mystery that we neglect to live according to the reality.

WHAT DOCTRINES ARE PART OF POSITIONAL TRUTH?

Justification by faith is the most important positional doctrine because it is critical to having a healthy view of the Christian life. It is the central doctrine of two books in the New Testament—Romans and Galatians. This doctrine is the subject of the next two Pocket Principles®.

We will also look at other doctrines that relate to our position in Christ. These include redemption (what it means to be bought with a price), reconciliation (what it means to be made right with God), and propitiation (what it means for Christ to pay the penalty for our sin). Each of these truths will add another dimension to what it means to be "in Christ" and will have implications for how we should live as Christians.

CONCLUSION

In his letter to the Ephesians, Paul urged them to live up to their calling (Ephesians 4:1). In other words, he was exhorting them to live up to who they really were in Christ Jesus. Of course, the only way for them to do this was to understand their position in Christ.

The same holds true for us today. Go back to Romans 12:1-2. How are we conformed to the image of Christ? By transforming our minds according to the truths of Scripture. We should make it a priority to study and understand positional truth so that we can live out these truths in our daily lives. Scripture tells us that we have been given tremendous spiritual riches in Christ. Let us take hold of positional truth and live like princes rather than like paupers!

Positional Truth

GOAL:

For a disciple to understand the difference between positional and experiential truth.

GETTING STARTED:

An ambassador is responsible to represent and speak for a certain country and that country's leadership. What are some of the privileges that come with being an "ambassador"?

STUDYING TOGETHER:

1. Based on your reading of Pocket Principle #1, how would you define "positional truth" and "experiential truth"?

    Positional Truth:

    Experiential Truth:

Read Ephesians 1:3-8.

2. What positional truths do you see in these verses?

3. According to Ephesians 1, what was God's motivation that causes Him to give us these spiritual blessings?

Read Ephesians 4:25-32.

4. What experiential truths do you see in these verses?

Read Galatians 3:1-5.

5. What is Paul warning the Galatians against?

Legalism is making works the basis of our relationship with Christ instead of accepting the positional truths by faith.

Read Galatians 3:14-15,23-25.

6. What is the basis of our relationship with Christ?

7. Describe the relationship between positional truth and experiential truth?

LOOKING AT REAL LIFE:

8. What effect would it have on an individual Christian if he understood positional truth?

9. How do you think it would affect Christians if the church they attended didn't teach positional truth, but only taught experiential truth?

10. How does positional truth conflict with our culture?

LOOKING AT MY LIFE:

Have you heard teaching about positional truth in the past?
How does understanding positional truth affect your life?

Justification By Faith: The Gospel

"And that's the gospel truth." So asserts the one who wants a listener or audience to believe that what he or she has to say is absolutely, undeniably true. Ironically, many who use this expression may have little idea of what the truth of the gospel actually is.

A study several years back suggests that this is true even among professing Christians. The October 1993 issue of *Moody Monthly* magazine relates the findings of a study which suggests widespread confusion about the gospel. George Barna, president of the Barna Research Group that conducted the study, is quoted as saying, "There is plenty of reason for churches to worry if nearly one-half of their people who believe in evangelism also believe in salvation by works."[1]

But what is the gospel truth? What is so important that it was foretold by prophets and angels for hundreds of years before Christ, then announced and visibly demonstrated by Jesus the promised Messiah, and now preached around the world for the two millennia since Jesus walked this earth? We will begin to explore this topic together. In this Pocket Principle™, we will focus on the truth of justification by faith and see how integral this truth is to the gospel message. Because justification by faith is such a critical doctrine, the rest of this series of Pocket Principles® will develop the meaning, benefits, and implications of this doctrine to Christians.

> The good news of the gospel would seem nonsensical or irrelevant if it were not for the bad news.

The Apostle Paul lays out the most extensive presentation of the gospel recorded in Scripture in the first five chapters of his letter to the Romans. In the early verses of this epistle, he establishes two points that set the stage for what is to follow. First, he introduces the gospel, saying that its message has the power to save all people who believe it (Romans 1:16). He then immediately introduces the heart of the gospel—justification—in the following verse by referring to a righteousness from God that is by faith.

We can understand how justification by faith fits into the gospel message by dividing the gospel into its parts. Some may react negatively to any effort to dissect the gospel, as though it were a laboratory rat or a machine that could be taken apart and studied piece by piece. This is a valid concern. The gospel is full of mystery; how can mystery be explained? The gospel is relational, not mechanical; how can relationships be studied this way? However, a clear understanding of the gospel actually highlights its relational aspects. By examining the various parts of the gospel, we will highlight rather than obscure its inherent relational nature, and we will gain a greater appreciation of the mysterious ways that God pursues a love relationship with us.

THE BAD NEWS—MANKIND'S HOPELESS CONDITION

It may seem in poor taste to start with bad news. However, the good news of the gospel would seem nonsensical or irrelevant if it were not for the bad news. The good news is necessary, relevant, and very good news indeed because of the hopelessness and helplessness of the bad news.

The first point to understand about the bad news is that people are sinful and separated from God. God's standard is His own holiness and righteousness. "Be holy because I, the LORD your God, am holy," said God to His people (recorded by Moses in Leviticus 19:2 and repeated by Peter in I Peter 1:14-16). "Yeah, right," one might be tempted to say in exasperation or disbelief. Yet, that is indeed the standard.

To make this standard more practical and understandable, God communicated specific commands that are in accordance with His holiness. However, all this revelation did was to highlight our inadequacy, which was exactly God's point. He gave the law to provide a measure that would show humans that they have fallen short of the divine standard and that they need a savior (Romans 3:19-23). As Romans 3:20 points out, "The law simply shows us how sinful we are." (*New Living Translation*)

> It is ludicrous for any of us to think that we could begin to measure up to God's perfect standard of righteousness.

This statement applies to every human being. Romans 3:23 states bluntly, "For all have sinned and fall short of the glory of God." Some might sin more, some might sin less; it doesn't matter—all have sinned, and all fall short of God's perfect standard. Many people don't accept this fact. They are convinced that God will grade on the curve. They think that when God lines them up next to their neighbor, coworker, ex-spouse, or whomever, they will fare pretty well. While this line of thinking may seem logical, it is fatally flawed for it is not in accordance with the truth revealed in Scripture.

A useful way to understand this dynamic is to think about a long-distance swimming contest. A large group of swimmers line up on the coast of California, ready to compete to see who can get to Hawaii first. A number of swimmers, in poor condition and not able swimmers to begin with, make it only a hundred yards or so from shore. Perhaps a larger group, younger and in better shape, swim out several hundred yards before the constant onslaught of the waves wears them out. Only a small handful make it farther than that. And even the best swimmer, one who has trained for years and is in peak physical condition, can swim for no more than several miles in these conditions. What is that compared to the several thousand miles of water that lie between California and

Hawaii? It's ridiculous to even conceive of such a contest. Just so, it is ludicrous for any of us to think that we could begin to measure up to God's perfect standard of righteousness.

Even one sin compromises a person's otherwise perfect record.

God's law demands perfection. According to James, the brother of Jesus, to fail at one point of the law is to fail at the whole (James 2:10). Some may not think it fair that a person should be judged guilty of the whole law if she only falls short in one point. But just as one broken link compromises an otherwise strong chain, so even one sin compromises a person's otherwise perfect record. In one respect, the argument is pointless because, indeed, none of us can claim to have fallen short at one point only.

In Romans 3:9-18, Paul paints a dreadful, yet realistic portrait of sinful people. He quotes repeatedly from Old Testament passages to emphasize his point that all are sinners. There is no relativism or comparative language here; rather, the absoluteness of these words is striking:

All people…are under the power of sin. As the Scriptures say,
"No one is righteous—not even one.
No one is truly wise; no one is seeking God.
All have turned away; all have become useless.
No one does good; not a single one." (NLT)

The second main point of the bad news is that our sin places us in eternal peril, and there is nothing that we can do to change our situation or save ourselves. We are guilty of breaking God's law, and the judicial penalty for breaking God's law is death (Romans 6:23).

Not only are sinful people under the sentence of death, but they also have neither the will nor the ability to save themselves. They are blinded by Satan to their predicament and to the truth of the gospel (II Corinthians 4:4), and they are enslaved to their own sin (Romans 6:17). Such is their condition that, if God did not show mercy and do something to help, they would certainly die in their sins and spend eternity apart from God.

THE GOOD NEWS—GOD'S INCREDIBLE SOLUTION

The good news is that God has done something! Knowing that we could do nothing to save ourselves, God took the initiative and provided a way of salvation. God Himself entered our world (space and time) in the person of Jesus. He lived a sinless life among us and became a perfect human substitute for us by dying in our place (I Peter 3:18). By His sinless death, Jesus took our place and our punishment and satisfied God's righteous wrath against sin. Using rich, figurative language, the prophet Isaiah described what the Lord did for us by describing Him as a sacrificial lamb that was led to slaughter (Isaiah 53:4-10). This image would have been familiar to his listeners as the entire Old Testament sacrificial system had been designed by God as an object lesson to explain the truths of the gospel.

Because Christ paid the penalty for our sins, we can be forgiven for them (Colossians 2:13). But, amazingly, God offers more than just forgiveness for our sins. He also offers to declare us righteous (justified) in His sight, that is, to give us right standing with Him. He does this by transferring our sin to Christ and Christ's righteousness to us (II Corinthians 5:21). This is the great doctrine of justification by faith, which is the central teaching of both Romans and Galatians and, in truth, of the entire Bible. As we have noted before, this doctrine is the most important positional truth taught in Scripture, and we will explore it in greater depth in succeeding Pocket Principles®.

MANKIND'S RESPONSE—REPENTANCE AND FAITH

Repentance and faith comprise the only appropriate response to the bad news. Each response is essential. Repentance without faith is simply remorse. Faith without repentance is empty, completely inconsistent with the message that must be believed.

What is true, biblical repentance? A good example is provided in Acts chapter 2 where Peter is found preaching to the crowds gathered on the day of Pentecost. Peter charged the crowd and their religious leaders with crucifying the Messiah. This is not exactly the way to win friends and influence people! However, the Holy Spirit brought great conviction on the crowd, and they cried out as one, "What shall we do" to be saved?

Notice first what Peter did not *say*. He did not tell the crowd that they needed to get their act together. He did not tell them that they needed to do penance for their evil deeds. And he did not tell them that they only needed to feel remorse or sorrow. The crowd was under such conviction at this point that, conceivably, they would have done whatever Peter asked of them. But instead of laying harsh demands on them and exacting a "pound of flesh" in revenge for their brutality (and his shame), Peter simply told them to do what is at once the easiest and yet the hardest thing to do. "Repent" Peter charges the crowd.

Repentance conveys the idea of a person who is walking down the street and realizes that she is headed in the wrong direction. Not only does she stop walking in the wrong direction, but also she turns and is willing to walk in the right direction. However, even though she is willing, she is unable to walk in the right direction without God's power.

Repentance without faith is simply remorse.

The word used in the New Testament for repentance—*metanoeo*—literally means a "change of thinking." When a person repents, she changes her mind and does not want to continue in her sinful ways. Repentance means that a person is willing to change. Recognizing that she has no power in and of herself to change, she is willing to let God change her.

Faith is also a necessary response to the good news of the gospel. By faith, we turn to God, take Him at His Word and trust His willingness and ability to save us. This faith is grounded in the finished work of Christ on the cross. It is the belief that God has provided a way for us to come back into full relationship with Him. Thus, repentance and faith are essential parts of the same act because as I turn away from sin (repent), I turn to Christ (faith).

Given people's lost condition, no one can come unless God draws her (John 6:44). But this is God's intent. People cannot come to belief unless the Holy Spirit convicts them of sin and convinces them that the gospel message is true. This is the business the Holy Spirit is in (John 16:8).

CONCLUSION

God, in His great mercy, has provided the way for restoration of fellowship between Himself and humans. He has done for us what we could not do for ourselves. No wonder the gospel is called the good news! No wonder it is the greatest story ever told! May we wonder anew at this greatest of all gifts from the loving hands of our Creator.

End Note:

1. George Barna, *Moody Monthly* (Moody Press, October 1993), 93.

Justification By Faith: The Gospel

GOAL:

For a disciple to understand the centrality of the doctrine of justification by faith to the gospel.

GETTING STARTED:

You are a newspaper journalist, writing an article. There is one central idea that you want to communicate. How would you go about doing that?

STUDYING TOGETHER:

1. Based on your reading of Pocket Principle #2, how would you define "justification by faith"?

In order to understand the significance of justification by faith, we must first understand the condition of humans after the Fall.

Read I Peter 1:14-16.

2. According to these verses, what is God's standard for us?

3. What is "holiness"?

Read Romans 3:9-20,23.

4. How does Paul describe the condition of humans as a result of the Fall?

5. What is the dilemma that non-Christians face according to these verses?

God has looked at the non-Christian's dilemma and has provided <u>justification</u> as a solution, which is God declaring the person righteous based on Christ's righteousness.

Read Romans 3:21-22.

6. What part does righteousness play in God's solution to this dilemma?

7. What does a person need to do to access this righteousness?

LOOKING AT REAL LIFE:

8. What are some ways people in our culture try to make themselves acceptable and righteous?

9. Why do people want to earn their own righteousness?

10. Many people believe that if their good deeds outweigh their bad, they will go to heaven. What is wrong with this belief?

    What does Christianity teach about what qualifies us to go to heaven?

11. Ephesians 2:8-9 says, "For it is by grace you have been saved, through faith— and this is not from yourselves, it is the gift of God—not by works, so that no one can boast." What would you say to explain this verse to a young Christian?

LOOKING AT MY LIFE:

What are the benefits to you personally right now of knowing that the only basis of your acceptance by God is Christ's righteousness?

Are you experiencing these benefits in your life now? Why or why not?

The Meaning Of Justification

What is our greatest need? Philosophers and sages down through the centuries have debated this question. Some behavioral scientists, such as Abraham Maslow, have developed models that put needs into different categories. Most would agree on the basics—we need such things as air, food, and water just to survive. However, once basic physical needs have been met, there is disagreement about what we need most. The Bible states plainly that our greatest needs are spiritual.

People need forgiveness for their sins. They need to be made right with God. Justification—the basis for right standing and relationship with God—is required for eternal life and is essential for living this life in the way that God intends. In his book *Knowing God*, noted theologian James I. Packer suggests that justification is the primary blessing because it meets our primary need. Martin Luther, the 16th century German monk whose 95 theses sparked the Protestant Reformation, refers to justification in his commentary on Galatians as, "the principle article of all Christian doctrine." [1]

> Justification is the primary blessing because it meets our primary need.

One might think that this principle article of doctrine would constantly remain at the forefront of the church's teaching. Sadly, this has not always been the case. The church has lost track of this doctrine for long periods of time in the past (in fact, Martin Luther's and others' reaction to a "works-based" righteousness was the entire basis of the Protestant reformation). At other times, the church has vigorously debated the importance of this doctrine. When justification is not emphasized, the church and individual Christians tend to fall back into legalism, that is, the belief that our acceptance with God is determined by our works instead of by Christ's righteousness.

Mini reformations are necessary any time the church begins to lose its emphasis on salvation by faith alone. In fact, personal reformations may be necessary when Christians forget that they have been saved by grace and begin to try to work on their standing before God. The church and individual Christians need to maintain a definite focus on this doctrine in order to avoid error and to develop into healthy and mature Christians. We can gain a clearer understanding of the meaning of justification by studying several important words and concepts.

THE MEANING OF KEY BIBLICAL WORDS

"Justification" and "righteousness" are two words that must be understood. These words are closely related and, in fact, have the same root word in Koine Greek (the language the New Testament was written in). When used as an adjective or noun, this word is often translated as "righteous" or "righteousness." When used as a verb, it is often translated as "justify." Justification is simply "the act whereby God makes one righteous."

When we speak of justification in normal, daily conversation, we mean the basis or reason for a decision or action. When we ask how someone can justify a decision or action, we are asking how they can support it. A coach might be asked to justify his decision to leave the starting pitcher in the game, even when his pitches appear to be losing steam. A businesswoman might be asked her justification for pursuing a particular course of action. A parent might ask a child how he can justify his decision to place swimming ahead of schoolwork. Well, might we ask how God can justify His decision to declare sinners to be righteous. Justification does not mean that God looks the other way or simply ignores our sin; rather the sacrificial death of Jesus Christ provides the basis by which the perfect justice of God is satisfied (Romans 4:25).

Justification involves more than just the forgiveness of sins, although that is an important part of it. It means that a person is not only declared innocent, but also is declared righteous. Based on Christ's sacrifice on our behalf and His giving to us His righteousness, we are viewed as having met God's holy standard of perfection (II Corinthians 5:21; Philippians 3:9).

> *…that I may gain Christ and be found in Him, not having a righteousness of my own that comes from the law, but that which is through faith in Christ—the righteousness that comes from God on the basis of faith.* (Philippians 3:9)

> Justification means that a person is not only declared innocent, but also is declared righteous.

So we see then that justification is closely related to righteousness. Of course, this begs the question, what is righteousness? According to the dictionary, the origin of the word righteous means to move in a straight line. In other words, it means to measure up to a standard. From a moral perspective, righteous means living or acting in the right way. Justification and righteousness will be further explored in the context of the following key historical concepts.

FIVE HELPFUL CONCEPTS

The reformers (such as Luther and Calvin) drew several sharp contrasts between justification and sanctification—the progressive growth of the Christian—that highlight the importance of justification. As they wrestled with these concepts they came up with several descriptive phrases to explain the unique nature of justification.

Passive righteousness

The righteousness we receive is not gained by anything we do. We do nothing but simply receive it by faith. The reformers called this "passive righteousness."

In his book, *Your Father Loves You*, James I. Packer suggests that the analogy of new birth was used by Christ and used in Scripture to purposefully convey specific truths regarding salvation. He points out that just as an infant plays no role in his own conception and birth, so the Christian receives new birth (regeneration) as a gift rather than as something that he helped to bring about. It is something that happens to him; he does not make it happen. [2]

> The righteousness we receive is true because God declares it to be so.

The fact that justification is not something we achieve or earn has many implications for the Christian. Because it is pointless to spend our energy trying to become righteous, we can focus our energy on being righteous. Because we cannot earn justification, we cannot "un-earn" it. When the Christian fully grasps these truths, he is filled with humility, thankfulness, and confidence.

Alien righteousness

Closely related to the concept of "passive righteousness" is the idea of "alien righteousness." Justification is righteousness that does not have its origin in humans; it comes from a source outside ourselves. Its source is God Himself and, therefore, is called a righteousness from God (Romans 1:17, 3:21; Philippians 3:9). Because this righteousness is external to anything we possess naturally, the reformers referred to it as "alien righteousness."

The concept of "alien righteousness" strikes a blow against the common belief that we have everything we need in ourselves. Modern thinkers would have us believe that we just need to look deep within ourselves to find everything we need. The truth is that when we honestly look deep within ourselves, we realize only that we are sinful and needy. We need help from outside ourselves, and that is exactly what God provides.

Forensic righteousness

In his book *The Cross of Christ*, pastor and theologian John Stott points out that the many facets of salvation can be viewed as occurring in different venues. For example, the concept of propitiation (Christ's death paying the penalty for our sin) brings the imagery of the Old Testament Temple to mind. The idea of redemption takes us to the marketplace, where things can be bought back again by the original owner. Reconciliation, a key blessing of salvation, is presented against the backdrop of the family home. And justification, because it involves the pronouncement of our innocence, invokes the imagery of a court of law. The righteousness we receive is legal or judicial in nature and was referred to by the reformers as "forensic righteousness." [3]

In chapter 8 of the book of Romans, the apostle Paul provides a helpful perspective on the judicial nature of our righteousness. He states boldly in verse 1 that, "there is now no condemnation for those who are in Christ Jesus." Later he expands on this statement by asking rhetorically, "Who then is the one who condemns?" The only one with the right to condemn is God. However, He is the very one who has declared us innocent. He no longer condemns us because He has already condemned our sin in Christ (on the cross). God Himself has declared us not guilty, and there is no higher court to overturn the verdict.

Pastor and author Warren Wiersbe tells the story of an Englishman who went to the continent for a holiday. He owned a Rolls-Royce, considered by many to be the finest automobile ever made. Somewhere along the way, the man experienced mechanical problems with his car. He called the dealer back in England, and a mechanic was promptly dispatched to Europe to fix the car. Upon his return to England, the traveler wrote the dealer to find out how much he owed for repairs. To his surprise, he received a letter that said, "Dear Sir: There is no record anywhere in our files that anything ever went wrong with a Rolls-Royce." So it is with the Christian. Once the verdict of not guilty is rendered, there is no record of anything ever having gone wrong with us.

He is willing to give us His best when we bring Him our worst.

Declarative righteousness

The righteousness we receive is true because God declares it to be so. Using Abraham as an example of one who was justified by his faith in God, Paul writes, "And because of Abraham's faith, God counted him as righteous. And when God counted him as righteous, it wasn't just for Abraham's benefit. It was recorded for our benefit, too, assuring us that God will also count us as righteous if we believe in Him, the one who raised Jesus our Lord from the dead." (Romans 4:22-24, *NLT*) The reformers called this "declarative righteousness."

Imputed righteousness

The righteousness that is given to those who believe is the "righteousness of Christ." His righteousness is transferred or charged to the Christian's account. It is like a financial transaction where money is transferred from one account to another (Romans 4:3-4,22-24). The reformers called this "imputed righteousness."

This transaction has been referred to as The Great Exchange, and Scripture pictures it in several different ways. Evoking the image of a financial transaction, Paul writes to the Corinthian Christians: "For you know the grace of our Lord Jesus Christ, that though He was rich, yet for your sake He became poor, so that you through His poverty might become rich." (II Corinthians 8:9) In II Corinthians 5:21, Paul views the transaction as an exchange where our sins are put on Christ, and we receive back the righteousness of God. This verse states that, "God made Him [Jesus] who had no sin to be sin for us, so that in Him we might become the righteousness of God." Isaiah 64:6 reminds us that the best of our "righteous" acts are like filthy rags, but Christ takes them and gives us robes of righteousness (Isaiah 61:10).

> Righteousness is "instantaneous and complete, not piecemeal and gradual."

In each of these pictures, it would seem as though God gets a raw deal. We must remember that we do business on His terms. Such is His love for us and the value that He places on us that He is willing to give us His best when we bring Him our worst.

Several nights ago, we witnessed a total eclipse of the moon. This phenomenon occurs when the earth comes between the sun and the moon, completely blocking the path of the sun's light. The result is that the side of the earth facing the moon is cast into complete darkness. Living in the country far away from sources of artificial light, I was unable to see my hand in front of my face. This picture illustrates the truth of imputed righteousness, except that, in this case, the Son comes between God and the Christian. In other words, when God looks at me, He sees Christ.

CONCLUSION

At one point during his Sunday morning message a pastor asked, "How many of you are holy?" All he got in response was nervous titters and sheepish looks. Painfully aware of their shortcomings, none dared raise his hand. Yet, each Christian in attendance could have confidently and joyfully thrust his hand into the air. For indeed we have been made holy and righteous though our justification.

John Calvin, another of the reformers, in speaking about justification said that our righteousness is "instantaneous and complete, not piecemeal and gradual." Justification is the sole and complete basis of our relationship with God. We are righteous in His sight now and forever.

The words to a familiar hymn, *And Can It Be?*, written by Charles Wesley come to mind:

No condemnation now I dread;
Jesus, and all in Him, is mine;
Alive in Him, my living head,
And clothed in righteousness divine,
Bold I approach th'eternal throne,
And claim the crown, through Christ my own.

End Notes:

1. Martin Luther, *Commentary on the Epistle to the Galatians* (1535), Chapter 2, verse 13, Public Domain.

2. J.I. Packer, *Your Father Loves You: Daily Insights for Knowing God* (Shaw Books, 1986).

3. John Stott, *The Cross of Christ* (Downers Grove: InterVarsity Press, 1986).

The Meaning of Justification

GOAL:

For a disciple to gain a deeper appreciation for the doctrine of justification by faith.

GETTING STARTED:

When you were in school studying for an exam, how were you able to discern what the teacher thought was important and therefore would be on the exam?

STUDYING TOGETHER:

1. Please look at the box entitled "Definitions of Righteousness." The left column has words describing aspects of righteousness and the right column has definitions of righteousness. Match the two columns.

Definitions of Righteousness

a) Alien Righteousness	1) Righteousness we receive that is legal or judicial in nature. Refers to the pronouncement of a judge about guilt or innocence.
b) Passive Righteousness	2) Righteousness we receive from a source outside ourselves. It's righteousness from God.
c) Imputed Righteousness	3) Righteousness that is true because God declared it to be true.
d) Declarative Righteousness	4) Righteousness not gained by anything we have done. We receive it by faith.
e) Forensic Righteousness	5) Christ's righteousness is transferred to my account as a Christian. It's like a financial transaction in which money is transferred from one account to another.

2. Match the verses to the definitions of righteousness.

Verses describing Righteousness

a) Romans 3:21-22	1) Passive righteousness
b) Romans 4:4-5	2) Forensic righteousness
c) Romans 5:19	3) Imputed righteousness
d) II Corinthians 5:21	4) Alien righteousness

Note: Declarative righteousness does not have a specific verse associated with it, but it is inherent in the idea of righteousness.

Read II Corinthians 5:21.

3. This verse describes an exchange that takes place. What is the exchange?

4. Explain what you think John Calvin meant when he said righteousness is "instantaneous and complete, not piecemeal and gradual."

LOOKING AT REAL LIFE:

5. Given that righteousness is a gift (that is, we receive it from God and do nothing to earn it), how does understanding this affect the way you live the Christian life?

6. What part does guilt play in the lives of some Christians?

Read Romans 8:1.

7. In this verse Paul draws a conclusion based on the fact that we have been justified by faith. What does this verse say about this issue of guilt?

LOOKING AT MY LIFE:

What does it mean to you to "fully embrace and take advantage of the benefits of being justified by faith"? How are you doing this in your life? Explain your answer.

The Impact Of The Cross

The Leaning Tower of Pisa is one of the most famous buildings in the world for the simple reason that it is, in fact, leaning. This 179-foot tower, built in the 12th century A.D., leans a bit further each year and is now 17 feet out of plumb. Some scientists estimate that, within the next few years, the tower will lean too far over and will collapse. Not only is the tower built on less-than-stable ground (the word "pisa" means "marshy land"), but its foundation is only 10 feet deep. This well-known structure vividly illustrates the fact that a building is only as strong as its foundation. Likewise, a truth is only as strong and reliable as the foundation it is based on. Therefore, it is important for Christians to understand the foundation or basis of our justification.

Thankfully, this great truth rests upon a very stable foundation indeed. The Apostle Paul describes this foundation in verses 24 to 26 in the third chapter of his letter to the Romans, which reads as follows: "[All] are justified freely by His grace through the redemption that came by Christ Jesus. God presented Christ as a sacrifice of atonement, through the shedding of His blood—to be received by faith. He did this to demonstrate His righteousness, because in His forbearance He had left the sins committed beforehand unpunished— He did it to demonstrate His righteousness at the present time, so as to be just and the one who justifies those who have faith in Jesus."

A truth is only as strong and reliable as the foundation it is based on.

In a nutshell, the basis of justification is the sacrificial death of Jesus Christ upon the cross of Calvary, and all of the implications that flow from this earth-shattering event. Christ suffered a terrible ordeal on the cross in order to make it possible for us to have salvation and to be declared righteous. Christians can understand the basis of their justification by studying the following concepts that surround the cross of Christ.

THE REDEMPTION OF SINNERS

The first concept to note in these verses is that of redemption. The word "redemption" was a commercial term that had to do with the marketplace. Redemption referred to the cost of buying back something that had been lost or to pay a ransom for something that had been taken or sold (Leviticus 25:47-55). It was used particularly in the slave market to refer to the price of a slave. The word was usually used in a material sense; however Paul uses it in Romans 3 in a spiritual or moral sense.

Jesus paid a high price to ransom (redeem) us when He shed His blood and died for us (Mark 10:45). Peter emphasizes the price Christ paid when he writes, "For you know that God paid a ransom to save you from the empty life you inherited from your ancestors. And it was not paid with mere gold or silver, which lose their value. It was the precious blood of Christ, the sinless, spotless Lamb of God." (I Peter 1:18-19, *NLT*) When considering the price that was paid, it is important to note that Jesus paid the ransom to God, rather than to Satan. (Since Jesus is God, in effect God paid Himself.)

The following story has been told many times to illustrate the meaning of redemption. A boy carefully built a toy boat and painted it with bright, easily identifiable colors. He was proud of his creation but waited several days to make sure that the glue and paint had dried before he put it into the water. Finally, he took his prize possession down to the park and set it afloat in a stream. He squealed with delight as the boat bounced merrily along in the current. However, his joy turned to dismay as the current picked up speed and the boat began to drift out of sight. Try as he might, the boy could not catch up with his boat, and it was lost.

First He created us, then He redeemed us. We are twice His!

A few days later, the boy spotted his boat in the window of a toy store. He raced inside to claim his possession. He was shocked when the shopkeeper refused to let him have it. Someone had brought the boat to the store and sold it to the owner. The owner would only let the boy have it if he paid the purchase price. Determined to reclaim his prize, the boy ran home and broke open his bank. He returned to the toy store and purchased the boat. As he left the store with the boat firmly in his arms, he said, "Now you're twice mine. First, I made you and now I bought you." This simple story illustrates what God has done for us—first He created us, then He redeemed us. We are twice His!

There are several important implications of the high purchase price God paid for us.

- First, God was <u>willing to pay the price with His own son, Jesus Christ</u>. Pastor and teacher Warren Wiersbe relates that Martin Luther once read the account of Abraham offering Isaac on the altar in Genesis 22 for family devotions. His wife, Katie, said, "I do not believe it. God would not have treated His son like that!" "But, Katie," Luther replied, "He did." Although He is the creator and ruler of the universe and ultimately owns all things, it cost God a great deal to redeem us. There could be no higher demonstration of love than this act of sacrifice.

- Some Christians mistakenly believe that the only way we can emphasize the glory of God is to emphasize the lowliness and unworthiness of humans. Yet, by paying the price of our redemption—surely one of His most glorious acts—<u>God demonstrates that we have great value in His sight</u>. This value underscores the desire He has to bless us. As Paul points out in Romans 8:32, "He who did not spare His own Son but gave Him up for us all—how will He not also, along with Him, graciously give us all things?"

- Another implication that flows from redemption is that <u>the price was paid in full at Calvary</u>. Just before His final breath, Jesus cried out on the cross "It is finished." (John 19:30) The emphasis is on the completion of His mission. Jesus paid for all of our sins at the cross, even the ones not yet committed. Christ's sacrificial death made full payment for our sins; there is nothing left for us to add. This is why Paul could exult that we are justified freely by His grace (Romans 3:24).

- A final implication to consider is that because God redeemed us in this way, <u>He rightly owns us</u>. Paul affirms this point in his letter to the Christians at Corinth when he writes in the context of sexual purity, "You are not your own; you were bought at a price. Therefore honor God with your bodies." (I Corinthians 6:19b-20) God purchased us out of our slavery to sin to set us free to be under new ownership—a new slavery.

- Lest there be any doubt that <u>a transfer of allegiance is what God had in mind</u>, consider the words of Paul in II Corinthians 5:15: "And He [Christ] died for all, that those who live should no longer live for themselves but for Him who died for them and was raised again." However, this transfer of ownership does not create an unfair and burdensome situation, as it might at first appear. Rather, our new "slavery" sets us free to live as we were intended to live and is the only way we can ever realize ultimate meaning and purpose in life.

THE PROPITIATION FOR OUR SINS

A second major concept—that of propitiation—is found in verse 25 of Romans three where Paul writes, "God presented Christ as a sacrifice of atonement." The Greek word "hilasterion" that the *New International Version* renders as "a sacrifice of atonement" is translated by the *New American Standard* Bible as "propitiation." Neither of these words or phrases is very familiar to us. The footnote in the *NIV* helpfully provides an alternative translation of "the one who turns away wrath." The simplest word to translate "hilasterion" is "satisfaction." It is the idea that Jesus' death on the

> God purchased us out of our slavery to sin to set us free to be under new ownership— a new slavery.

cross was sufficient to satisfy God's wrath against sin—that is, Jesus turned away God's wrath.

The concept of atonement or satisfaction for sins was familiar to Paul's readers, particularly those who knew the Old Testament Scriptures. God instituted an elaborate sacrificial system for a number of reasons. A primary reason was to teach that there is a right way and a wrong way to approach a holy God. Another main reason was to use symbolism to teach truth. The offering of lambs without defect to atone for the sins of the people was a symbolic foreshadowing of the death of Jesus, the sinless Lamb of God.

Many people rightly see God as loving, understanding, and benevolent, but have trouble accepting that He is also holy, righteous, and just. His sense of right and wrong (justice) demands some kind of payment or retribution when wrong has been committed. Paul repeatedly touches on the fact of God's justice and wrath as he develops his line of argument in the book of Romans (Romans 1:18, 2:5, 2:8, 3:5).

Perhaps part of the reason some Christians have trouble accepting the concept of God's wrath is that we project our ways of anger and wrath onto Him. We are uncomfortable believing that God gets angry the way we do. And well we should be. John Stott writes in his book *The Cross of Christ*, "The wrath of God is His steady, unrelenting, unremitting, uncompromising antagonism to evil in all its forms and manifestations. In short, God's anger is poles apart from ours. What provokes our anger (injured vanity) never provokes His; what provokes His anger (evil) seldom provokes ours." [1]

Our new "slavery" sets us free to live as we were intended to live.

Since God's anger at sin has been satisfied, those who have trusted in Christ are at peace with God (Romans 5:1). It was our sin that separated us from God and puts us at enmity with Him. Christ's death provided the basis and opportunity for reconciliation between a holy God and sinful people. The cross has also become the basis to put to death the hostility people feel for their fellow humans. Once the vertical relationship has been restored, there is a strong basis for the restoration of horizontal relationships, particularly among fellow Christians. In Ephesians 2:14-18, Paul noted that Christ's death took away any reason for hostility between Jews and Gentiles. Surely this principle can be extended to all Christians, regardless of race, origin, or other factors that tend to divide us.

THE VINDICATION OF GOD'S JUSTICE

Christ's death on the cross also vindicates and validates the justice of God. Because God is just, He must exact a penalty for sin. This is why God required sacrifices for sin as part of the Old Testament system. However, the repeated offering of animal sacrifices could never take away sin, they could only provide a temporary cover for them (Hebrews 10:1-4). Paul makes this point in Romans 3:25 when he says, "in His [God's] forbearance He had left the sins committed beforehand unpunished." It took the once-and-for-all sacrifice of the sinless Son of God to take away sin.

God demonstrated His forbearance (willingness to withhold judgment) before the coming of the Messiah; He demonstrated His justice (willingness to execute judgment) by exacting the full penalty for sin and offering His own Son to bear the punishment on our behalf. As Paul writes in Romans 3:26, "He [God] did it to demonstrate His righteousness at the present time, so as to be just and the one who justifies those who have faith in Jesus."

CONCLUSION

Quoting again from Stott's *The Cross of Christ*: "It is God himself who in holy wrath needs to be propitiated, God himself who in holy love undertook to do the propitiating, and God himself who in the person of His Son died for the propitiation of our sins. Thus God took His own loving initiative to appease His own righteous anger by bearing it in His own self in His own Son when He took our place and died for us." [2] Truly we have an amazing God who remains true to Himself while providing a way of salvation for those who will turn to Him.

End Notes:

1. John Stott, *The Cross of Christ* (Downers Grove: InterVarsity Press, 1986), 173.

2. John Stott, 175.

The Impact Of The Cross

GOAL:

For a disciple to understand that the cross (the death and resurrection of Christ) is the basis of justification, and as such, impacts the Christian's relationship with God.

GETTING STARTED:

In our early education there are foundational concepts we learn that equip us for more advanced learning. What are some of these foundational concepts?

STUDYING TOGETHER:

Read Romans 3:24.

1. According to this verse, what brings about our justification?

2. What is redemption?

3. How did Jesus accomplish our redemption?

4. Jesus was willing to die for us; what does that say about us?

Read I Corinthians 6:18-20.

5. Verses 19b and 20 say, "You are not your own; you were bought at a price. Therefore honor God with your bodies." What are the implications for Christians?

Read Romans 3:25a.

In the *NIV* version of this verse Paul uses the phrase "sacrifice of atonement" which is translated "propitiation" in some other versions. This means that God's wrath has been satisfied.

6. How was God's wrath satisfied?

7. Why was it necessary to satisfy God's wrath?

Read Romans 3:25b-26.

8. How can God be both "just" and the "justifier"?

LOOKING AT REAL LIFE:

9. If God had not redeemed us and Jesus had not been our "sacrifice of atonement," what would be our state as Christians?

10. God has redeemed us, and Jesus was the sacrifice of atonement for us. What are some of the benefits of being His redeemed and atoned for children?

LOOKING AT MY LIFE:

Since God took the initiative and Jesus suffered the consequences (of our sin), what should be our response to Him? Is this your response? If not, meditate on Hebrews 10:1-14, and ask God to open your eyes to the incredible love He has shown to you through His sacrifice.

The Faith That Justifies

According to the *American Heritage Dictionary*, a gift is something that is "bestowed voluntarily and without compensation …" Most of us are familiar with the business practice of merchants sending coupons in the mail or placing them in newspapers or magazines offering a free gift to the recipient. The text usually emphasizes that no purchase is necessary; all one has to do to receive the gift is to call an 800 number or show up at the store to claim it.

Consider the above example and ask yourself the following question: Is a gift still a gift if something is required to receive it? Is the process of calling a telephone number or showing up at a store to receive a gift considered work or a payment for the gift? No, because originally no work was done in order for the gift to be offered. Redeeming the coupon is merely a way of receiving the gift. The gift is still "bestowed voluntarily and without compensation."

What about the free gift of salvation? Is faith a work that earns salvation or is it a way of receiving it? Faith is a way of receiving salvation that shows that the person wants to be justified before God. Not everyone who gets the mailing gets the gift; only those who want it enough to claim it get it. Just so, not everyone who is offered salvation receives it. God does not grant salvation indiscriminately, but only grants it to those who demonstrate that they want it through faith.

> Not everyone who is offered salvation receives it.

However, faith is more than just *another* way to receive salvation; it is the *only* way to receive salvation. As Paul writes in Romans 3:28, "We maintain that a person is justified by faith." And in Philippians 3:9, he describes his own hope to "be found in Him, not having a righteousness of my own that comes from the law, but that which is through faith in Christ—the righteousness that comes from God on the basis of faith." (See also Romans 1:16-17.)

Because this is true, it is important to understand the nature of faith. If faith is a work, then salvation is earned and Christianity is just one more works-based religious belief system. If faith is not a work, then what is it? The answer to this question is important because faith is one of the key elements of the Christian belief system. We can better understand the nature of the faith that justifies (or "saving faith") by studying the following ideas.

THE DEFINITION OF FAITH

Sometimes it is helpful to first consider what something is not in order to better understand what it is. Let's consider several ideas that help to define what faith is not.

<u>Faith is never just intellectual.</u>

Some mistakenly think that faith is simply a matter of mental assent or agreement with a particular truth or doctrine. Over the centuries, Christians have developed a number of creeds—carefully crafted statements of belief. These are important documents, and they remind us of and reinforce for us the truths that we hold dear. Yet even a non-Christian might pick up such a statement, read over it, and agree that the statement is true. Such agreement does not necessarily mean that the person is willing to put his trust in the God he is reading about. Faith involves the entire personality—mind, heart, and will. If the heart is not engaged and the will is not inclined, the mind alone cannot exercise faith. As James 2:19 reminds us, "You believe that there is one God. Good! Even the demons believe that—and shudder."

<u>Faith is never a blind leap in the dark.</u>

> Faith involves the entire personality— mind, heart, and will.

Others may attempt to denigrate faith as simple or childish. The phrase "a blind leap in the dark" is used to reinforce the perception of stupid or senseless following after something "that no one can really actually prove." Christians are accused of "checking their brains at the door" and hoping for "pie in the sky." Faith involves the entire personality— mind, heart, and will.

<u>Faith is never a work.</u>

Every belief system devised by humans is, at its core, a system of works-based righteousness. Whether it is a major religion such as Islam or Buddhism or a "Christian" cult such as the Mormons or Jehovah's Witnesses, the adherents to these systems are trying to work their way to "heaven," desperately hoping that they will be able to do enough to earn admittance.

Christianity stands in stark contrast to all other belief systems. Rather than people frantically trying to be good enough for God, it is God reaching down to people and providing salvation as a free gift. The very "freeness" of the gift is a stumbling block to many. They either think it's too good to be true or their pride tells them that they must earn their own way. In one of the cornerstone passages of Scripture, Paul writes, "For it is by grace you have been saved, through faith— and this is not from yourselves, it is the gift of God—not by works, so that no one can boast." (Ephesians 2:8-9)

We've looked at what faith is not; now let's view it from the other perspective and focus on some positive aspects of faith.

<u>While faith is never intellectual only, it does involve the intellect.</u>

True faith always requires an object. It is faith in something or someone. For the Christian, the faith that justifies or brings about salvation is trust in or reliance on Christ and what He has done for us. We must be able to grasp at least an elementary understanding of who Christ is and what He accomplished for us on the cross in order to put our faith in Him. Polls consistently show that a vast majority of Americans claim to have faith in God. Yet many of these people may not know anything about God or why they claim to have faith in Him. Essentially, their faith has no content and is worthless.

<u>While faith is never a blind leap in the dark, it does require going beyond the limits of our understanding.</u>

Augustine, one of the early church fathers, is quoted as saying, "God does not expect us to submit our faith to Him without reason, but the very limits of our reason make faith a necessity." The truth is that we can never really figure everything out. As Isaiah 55:9 reminds us, "As the heavens are higher than the earth, so are my ways higher than your ways and my thoughts than your thoughts." Hebrews chapter 11 is generally considered the greatest treatise of faith in Scripture. In the first verse, the writer describes faith as "confidence is what we hope for and assurance about what we do not see." For example, we weren't around at the creation of the world and most of us wouldn't claim to understand how God could speak things into being. Yet, by faith, we believe this (Hebrews 11:3). So while faith is not a blind leap in the dark, it is, as slain civil rights leader Martin Luther King, Jr. once said, "taking the first step even when you don't see the whole staircase."

> The very "freeness" of the gift [salvation] is a stumbling block to many.

<u>While faith is never a work, true faith does result in acts of obedience.</u>

Renowned Christian thinker and writer A.W. Tozer is quoted as saying, "The Bible recognizes no faith that does not lead to obedience, nor does it recognize any obedience that does not spring from faith. The two are opposite sides of the same coin."

The story is told of a man who fell off a cliff, but managed to grab a tree limb on the way down. The following conversation ensued: "Is anyone up there?" "I am here. I am the Lord. Do you believe me?" "Yes, Lord, I believe. I really believe, but I can't hang on much longer." "That's all right, if you really believe you have nothing to worry about. I will save you. Just let go of the branch." A moment of silence, then: "Is anyone else up there?" (Taken from *Bits & Pieces*, June 24, 1993). This humorous interchange reminds us that faith is proven to be genuine only when it is put into action.

The first act of obedience is that of unreservedly committing ourselves to Christ. In essence, we are surrendering control of our life to Him. Unless we are willing to do this, we do not have true, saving faith that results in justification. Such reliance on Christ implicitly involves a radical and total commitment to Him as our Lord. A person goes from "I'm going to follow my own path" to "I'm going to follow God." From "I'm going to trust in myself" to "I'm going to trust in God."

Paul describes this as an exchange of slaveries—from slavery to sin to slavery to God or righteousness (Romans 6:17-22). Just as slavery to sin results in certain actions, so also slavery to righteousness will result in certain actions. This is the point James was making to his readers when he wrote that faith without works is dead (James 2:17). James' position is often understood to contradict Paul's statement that faith is not a work, but such is not the case. He was simply presenting the flip side of the coin, as described by Tozer above.

THE ROLE OF GOD IN FAITH

Humans are so hopelessly lost (Ephesians 2:1-3,12) and blinded by Satan (II Corinthians 4:4) that they will not come to Christ and trust in Him for salvation if they are left to themselves (Romans 3:10-11). As Paul pointed out by quoting from Isaiah, there is no one (left to himself) who seeks after God (Romans 3:11). Paul's description of "without hope and without God in the world" (Ephesians 2:12) paints a pathetic yet accurate picture of the plight of the person who has not yet trusted Christ for salvation.

However, the good news is that God intervenes in the lives of people so that they can respond to His offer. The faith that we exercise is a gift of God; we respond in faith to His loving initiative. Jesus taught that no one would come to Him unless the Father drew him first (John 6:44). However, that was part of Jesus' mission—to draw others to Himself. Repeatedly throughout the Gospels, we see Jesus revealing Himself to people and inviting them to believe in Him. Jesus also taught that when He left this world to return to the Father, He would send the comforter—the Holy Spirit—to carry on His work and, specifically, to convict the world of what is really true (John 16:8-11).

The choice a person makes to exercise faith is in response to God's gracious offer—it also is a gift from God because of His initiative. Quoting Ephesians 2:8 again, "For it is by grace you have been saved, through faith...it is the gift of God." Theologians differ on the antecedent of "it" in the phrase "it is the gift of God." Does "it" refer to grace, to faith, or to the resulting salvation? Apparently, the grammatical structure could support multiple interpretations. While precision is always important when handling Scripture, in one sense it doesn't matter if we are unable to identify the antecedent with certainty because all three are true. Salvation, grace, faith—all are gifts of God.

AN EXAMPLE OF FAITH IN ACTION

In Romans 4, Paul presents Abraham, the "father" of the Jews, as a model of faith that brings about justification. The points that Paul makes regarding Abraham and his faith track closely with the ideas we've considered above.

Abraham's faith had an object. Not only did Abraham believe in God, he believed specific things about God and promises from God. He believed that God would give him offspring, even though he was old and his wife Sarah was beyond the age of childbearing. Abraham believed that God would show him where to go when He asked him to leave his own country. And he believed that God could raise the dead, so he was willing to offer his son Isaac to God.

Abraham moved out beyond his understanding. Abraham did not take a blind leap in the dark, but he did pack up and leave his own country. Surely he was ridiculed by family and friends who could not believe that a wealthy, established man would leave all this behind to follow God, and even did not know where God was taking him. Abraham certainly did not understand everything God was trying to do in his life, but he did understand the call of God and he obeyed it.

Abraham's faith resulted in obedience. On the command of God, he circumcised himself and the males in his family. He packed up and left his country for a land God had promised to show him. He offered his son Isaac on the altar. Doubtless there were countless acts of obedience along Abraham's journeys that did not get recorded in Scripture. But we do know that his life pattern was one of obedience.

Faith is proven to be genuine only when it is put into action.

However, it is important to remember that it was not his works that justified Abraham, but rather it was the faith that preceded the works. Paul is precise at this point. He states specifically that God accepted Abraham's faith first and then later Abraham was circumcised (Romans 4:10). Paul goes so far as to state that Abraham is the father of all who have faith but have not yet been circumcised. Circumcision was simply an outward symbol of the faith that Abraham had already placed in God (similar to the symbol of baptism for Christians today).

Paul also points out that Abraham was not justified by keeping the law (Romans 4:13). He says that if Abraham could have been justified by living according to law, then faith would be worthless. Rather, it was Abraham taking God at His word that was credited to him for righteousness (Genesis 15:6; Romans 4:22). The example of Abraham shows that salvation and justification occurred the same way in the Old Testament as in the New Testament, and that is by faith.

CONCLUSION

God, the great initiator, the Hound of Heaven (as C. S. Lewis was fond of saying) pursues us and invites us to enter relationship with Him. This relationship can only be entered into by faith. When we turn to God in faith, He grants us salvation and justification as free gifts.

Paul reminds the Christians in Colosse that they are to continue living the Christian life the same way that they began it—and that is by faith (Colossians 2:6). Or, to put it another way, we have a righteousness "that is by faith from first to last." (Romans 1:17) What a great God we have—one who freely gives us these good gifts. We can join the Apostle Paul in saying, "Thanks be to God for His indescribable gift!" (II Corinthians 9:15)

The Faith That Justifies

GOAL:

For a disciple to understand the faith that is necessary for justification.

GETTING STARTED:

Faith is necessary in many areas of life beyond spiritual matters. Give examples.

STUDYING TOGETHER:

Read Romans 3:21-22.

1. What role does faith play in justification?

Read Ephesians 2:8-9 and Romans 3:27-28, 4:1-5.

2. According to these verses, explain the difference between faith and works?

Read Romans 6:17-22.

3. According to these verses, what are some of the results of true faith?

Read Genesis 12:1-3 and 15:1-6.

4. Abraham believed the promises that God had made to him, and he was declared righteous because of this faith. What promises did Abraham believe?

Read Romans 4:18-24.

5. In this passage, how does Paul describe Abraham's faith?

6. In Romans 4 Paul not only explains that by faith Abraham was justified, he also points out some of the common misbeliefs about how people are made right with God. In the 3 passages listed below, what are the 3 misbeliefs Paul identifies? What is the error?

   Read Romans 4:1-5.

   Read Romans 4:9-12.

   Read Romans 4:13-15.

LOOKING AT REAL LIFE:

7. What are some common misbeliefs that people have today about what makes them right with God (gives them salvation)?

8. What role does going to church, giving, being baptized, praying, serving others, etc. play in the life of a Christian?

LOOKING AT MY LIFE:

Have you ever put your faith (believed) in something that cannot save (justify) you? Explain your answer.

What are you putting your faith in now?

The Benefits Of Our Justification

For the past several years, I (Jon) have been privileged to work for a company consistently ranked in the top ten of *Fortune* magazine's list of the "Best Places to Work in America." A number of factors go into this ranking. Benefits—such as time off, insurance, and retirement income—are important. So also is company culture, including how people are treated, the quality of communication, levels of trust, and so on. The end result for a company such as the one I work for is that nine out of ten employees agree that it is a great place to work.

I wonder what the numbers would look like if a survey were taken of professing Christians asking, "Do you believe that the Christian life is a great way to live?" I fear that a number of Christians would indicate that they are glad they won't be going to hell, but other than that, they don't see that the Christian life has much to offer. Even though most wouldn't be so bold as to state it quite that way, their attitudes and actions give them away. To them, Christ's bold claim that, "I have come that they may have life, and have it to the full," (John 10:10b) is just another mysterious saying, without much relevance to us today.

Perhaps many Christians do not embrace or live the abundant life because they do not fully understand the implications of their salvation. It is tremendously important that Christians gain an appreciation for and take advantage of the benefits of our justification as outlined in Romans 5:1-2. These benefits include a restored relationship with God, a privileged standing with God, and a certain future with Him.

A RESTORED RELATIONSHIP WITH GOD

Studies consistently show that a worker's relationship with her direct supervisor is often the most important factor in job satisfaction. While pay, working conditions, and other benefits are important, generally an employee will not be happy in her work if she does not have an open, healthy relationship with her boss. This kind of relationship is the number one predictor of a satisfied, motivated employee, and the absence of it is the number one reason why people leave their jobs.

Our justification provides the way for us to have an open, healthy relationship with God, our new Lord and Master. Many would view this as the primary benefit of our salvation—it is the reason Christ died to save us, and it is the basis for all other blessings.

Paul writes in Romans 5:1, "Therefore, since we have been justified through faith, we have peace with God through our Lord Jesus Christ." In these few words he touches on the need for, the basis of, and the results of a new relationship with God.

The need for a new relationship

The Christian needs a new relationship with God because, prior to our salvation, we were at enmity with God. Or, to put it more bluntly, we were God's enemy (Colossians 1:21). Some of us may have a hard time understanding this. We perhaps do not appreciate our new relationship with God because we do not now remember or did not then grasp the seriousness of our former condition.

Our previous condition was not just that of a strained relationship with God. The relationship was severed, with no apparent means of re-connection. As John Milne reminds us in his book *Know the Truth*, "the way back to Eden is barred by a flaming sword."

God is always ready to be reconciled to people. It is people who turned their backs on God.

What we might want to write off as ignorance or indifference, God views as hostility. As Jesus pointed out to the religious leaders of His day, "whoever is not with me is against me." (Matthew 12:30) As non-Christians, we were under the control of our sinful nature, which is always hostile to God (Romans 8:7-8). We had no desire to obey God's laws and could not obey even if we wanted to. As Paul explains in Romans 2:5-8, the result of our sin and hostility was that God was prepared to direct His wrath toward us, had we not accepted the pardon He offered.

The basis for a new relationship

Second Corinthians 5:21 states that, "God made Christ, who never sinned, to be the offering for our sin, so that we could be made right with God through Christ." (*NLT*) The basis for peace with God is Christ's death on the cross. Jesus experienced the wrath of God against sin, so that our sentence of condemnation could be removed. He provided the way for us to be reconciled to God (Romans 5:10-11).

Reconciliation emphasizes the removal of hostility between two persons, in this case between God and people. Notice that Scripture never speaks of God being reconciled to people; it is always the other way around. The fact is that God has never needed to be reconciled to people because He has never done anything to breach the relationship. However, He initiates and creates the conditions for reconciliation. It is our choice to respond to God's gracious offer of forgiveness and reconciliation by placing our faith in Christ Jesus.

God is always ready to be reconciled to people. It is people who turned their backs on God, yet it is God who is always patiently waiting and willing to forgive. Sadly, many stubbornly refuse to accept His forgiveness. Although the analogy is limited, it is in some ways similar to a couple that has experienced marital difficulties due to the husband's infidelity. The wife may be willing to forgive the husband and desire reconciliation. However, until he is willing to accept her forgiveness (and turn from his sin!), reconciliation is impossible.

The results of a new relationship

A restored relationship—peace with God—has several implications. This peace creates great "working conditions" in our relationship with God. Sin was a harsh taskmaster, always beating us down, keeping us defeated, and taking a toll in every area of our lives. The Christian now has a kind and gracious master, one who is a joy to work for.

Peace with God also gives us a sense of freedom and confidence. This is not a fragile truce that might be broken at any time. Our peace with God is permanent and abiding. As we noted earlier, peace is a result of our justification. And our justification is the result of the saving work of Christ on the cross. So it does not depend on us; it depends on God. We may fail, we may falter, we may change, but our new relationship with God is secure. He has welcomed us into this place of reconciliation, and He will not rescind the invitation.

> To stand in grace is to enjoy all the riches God has to offer.

A further implication is that, having made peace with God, we can now act as agents of His peace with others. In fact, it is our privilege and our obligation to serve as Christ's ambassadors and plead with others to be reconciled to God (II Corinthians 5:18-20).

A PRIVILEGED STANDING WITH GOD

A second major benefit of our justification, and one that flows from the first, is that we enjoy a new standing with God. Paul writes in Romans 5:2 that, "we have gained access by faith into this grace in which we now stand." This goes beyond a simple ending of hostilities. Not only are we no longer God's enemies, but He graciously welcomes us to dwell in His presence as His children.

Grace is "undeserved blessing." Some people remember the Christian meaning of grace by making GRACE an acrostic—God's Riches At Christ's Expense. God is not miserly with His grace. Paul writes in Galatians that, because we are God's children, everything He has belongs to us (Galatians 4:7). To stand in grace is to enjoy all the riches God has to offer. The *New Living Translation* renders our standing as "this place of undeserved privilege" and that is indeed what it is. (Romans 5:2)

Just as we don't have to worry about our peace with God being broken, we don't have to worry about His grace being withdrawn. It is not earned, and it cannot be "un-earned." That is why popular Christian artist Kathy Troccoli can sing of God's stubborn love—"a love that never lets go of me." (From *Stubborn Love* Album) Grace is our constant and abiding experience. Although experientially it may seem more available or more real at certain times, the truth is that we stand in it all the time.

> The truth is that we have, at best, a limited understanding of what heaven will be like.

In some small way, this access can be compared to the Open Door policy that many leading companies boast of. In these companies, employees supposedly have the right to go into their boss's office at any time and ask any question. If they don't get satisfaction from their immediate supervisor, they have the right to continue to the next level. Some companies have set up formal systems where employees can ask questions directly of the president, either in person or by e-mail. However, it's one thing to have such a stated policy; it is quite another for employees to truly believe that it is safe to go through the open door, to know that they will be treated with dignity and respect, and to believe that their concerns will be taken seriously.

Yet that is exactly the privilege we now have through Christ. The writer of Hebrews says that we can boldly approach God in our time of need and find grace (Hebrews 4:16). Why do we come boldly? Because, for the Christian, it is a throne of grace rather than a throne of judgment. We come "assured of His glad welcome" as Paul writes in Ephesians 3:12 (*Living Bible*). God stands ready to deal with us in a gracious way, but many times we don't experience His grace because we do not approach Him. As James points out, "You do not have because you do not ask God." (James 4:2)

Romans 8:31-32 summarizes God's new posture toward us by asking a series of rhetorical questions: "What, then, shall we say in response to these things? If God is for us, who can be against us? He who did not spare His own Son, but gave Him up for us all—how will He not also, along with Him, graciously give us all things?" Surely, we stand in a place of grace and of abundance.

A CERTAIN FUTURE WITH GOD

A third major benefit of our justification is that we are assured of a future with God. Paul writes in Romans 5:2b that, "we boast in the hope of the glory of

God." Hope as used here does not indicate a hopeful stance but rather a certain expectation. The *NLT* renders this phrase as "we confidently and joyfully look forward to sharing God's glory."

Although the abundant life begins now, it does not end at death. In fact, life is really just beginning. In current slang, when one is terribly impressed with something and wants to give it the highest compliment, she might say that it is "a car to die for" or "a stereo to die for." Christians have a retirement plan "to die for."

Though it is our final rest in Christ that we look forward to, it will not really be retirement. Rather, it will be something of a "working retirement." We will have all the time in the world to do what we were created for—to worship God and to enjoy His presence forever (in the words of the *Westminster Catechism*).

The idea of an eternal church service doesn't necessarily excite a lot of Christians. That may say something about the typical Sunday morning worship service. It probably says more about our lack of understanding of what it really means to worship God and to live in His presence. The truth is that we have, at best, a limited understanding of what heaven will be like.

We do know that we will receive new and perfect bodies. This truth should come as a relief to some of us who wonder whether the bodies we have now can hold out for the duration of our earthly sojourn. Our new bodies will be full of glory and of power (I Corinthians 15:42-49). These bodies will be given to us so that we can enjoy a meaningful existence.

We are told we will rule with Christ, even though we may not understand exactly what that means. We are also told that we will receive rewards in heaven based on what we have done while on earth (I Corinthians 3:12-15), which seems to indicate that some have more to look forward to than others (although it is hard to imagine anyone being disappointed).

> The Christian's "retirement plan" is secure. We are declared righteous for eternity.

We can echo the wonder of the child that author Charles Allen writes about in *Home Fires*. She was taking an evening walk with her father. Wonderingly, she looked up at the stars and exclaimed; "Oh, Daddy, if the wrong side of heaven is so beautiful, what must the right side be!" [1] We would be thrilled to inherit or win great riches here on earth, but this is nothing in comparison to the riches God has waiting for us in heaven (I Peter 1:3-9). Small wonder that Paul writes in Romans 5:2 that we rejoice ("exult" or leap for joy) in our hope of glory.

Most companies have moved away from "defined benefit" plans (receive a set amount each month in retirement) to "defined contribution" plans (receive a set amount toward your retirement). However, even with a defined contribution plan, there is no guarantee of a substantial retirement benefit. With the volatility of the stock market in recent years and with a number of large companies going bankrupt, many have seen their retirement savings dwindle significantly or disappear. Thankfully, the Christian's "retirement plan" is secure. Justification is God's judgment of Christians at salvation. It is God declaring us righteous now, not waiting until the judgment day. Therefore, our future is secure. We are declared righteous for eternity.

Our secure hope of glory also provides perspective on our current situation. We are better able to deal with the pain and difficulties of this life, which often seem endless, when we view them in the light of eternity. Paul writes that our present trials and struggles, which often cloud our perspective, are only light and momentary afflictions compared to the eternal weight of glory waiting for us in heaven (II Corinthians 4:17).

CONCLUSION

John Stott, in his commentary on Romans titled *Men Made New*, sums up Romans 5:1-2 as follows: "Here are the fruits of our justification—peace, grace, and glory. Peace with God (which we have), grace (in which we stand), and glory (for which we hope)." He goes on to point out that these three characteristics represent the immediate, the ongoing, and the ultimate effects of our justification. [2]

What should our response be to these benefits of justification? We should take advantage of a new harmonious relationship with God by enjoying time with Him. We should take advantage of the constant availability of God's grace and favor by approaching Him with boldness and confidence. And, in light of our future hope, we should live as sojourners in this world. We can travel light and refuse to wear ourselves out in the rat race, knowing that our true reward awaits us in heaven.

End Notes:

1. Charles L. Allen, *Home Fires: A Treasury of Wit and Wisdom* (1987).

2. John Stott, *Men Made New* (Downers Grove: InterVarsity Press, 1966), 12.

The Benefits Of Our Justification

GOAL:

For a disciple to understand the faith that is necessary for justification.

GETTING STARTED:

Consider a person who goes on a luxury cruise and instead of enjoying cruise activities, stays in her cabin watching TV during the entire cruise. What might be some reasons she isn't taking advantage of the available activities that are included in the price of the cruise—activities such as dining, entertainment, ocean view, etc.?

STUDYING TOGETHER:

Read Romans 5:1-2.

1. What are the benefits Paul lists in these verses?

2. What does it mean to have peace with God?

Read Colossians 1:21-22.

3. What was our former condition, and what is the evidence of it?

4. How did God resolve this problem, and what was the result?

5. In Romans 5:2 we read that we as Christians stand in grace. Define "grace."

    What kind of picture does standing in grace bring to mind?

Romans 5:2b says we have hope for a future.

Read II Corinthians 4:17; Ephesians 2:6-7 and I Peter 1:3-4.

6. According to these verses, what does God say about our future (in the next life)?

LOOKING AT REAL LIFE:

7. What are some things that might prevent a Christian from experiencing grace?

8. What is the effect of a Christian knowing that she always stands in grace in her relationship with God?

9. How does knowing that she will go to heaven and have a closer relationship with God impact the Christian's life in the present?

LOOKING AT MY LIFE:

In this study we have looked at 3 benefits of our justification: peace with God, grace and hope for the future. Which of these benefits is the most meaningful to you right now and why?

Grace And Sin

Augustine of Hippo, considered one of the early Church fathers, lived in the fourth and fifth centuries AD. Rescued by God from a life of debauchery, he became a devoted follower of Christ. His writings demonstrate this devotion, as well as his keen understanding of the truth of the gospel. At one point, Augustine wrote that the natural outworking of the doctrine of justification could be summed up as, "Love God, and do as you please." Had Augustine been a contemporary of the Apostle Paul, this quote would have provided ammunition to Paul's critics. "So you see," they would have charged, "this Augustine has read your letters and has found a basis to continue his life of sin." "Quite the opposite," Paul might have replied, "Augustine has found grace and can now live a life pleasing to God."

Because of his teaching on the grace of God, Paul had his critics. They expressed concern that Christians would take advantage of grace, free choice, and God's forgiveness in order to continue in sin and to sin even more than before. In the opening verses of Romans 6, Paul pre-empts their criticism by asking rhetorically, "What shall we say then? Are we to continue in sin so that grace may increase?" "May it never be!" (*NASB*) He thunders in response to his own question. Then he goes on to explain his answer. It is important to note that Paul never apologized for his teaching on grace or tried to water it down. Rather, he showed why a true understanding of grace never leads to careless and sinful living but rather always leads toward a life of holiness and devotion to God.

> A true understanding of grace…always leads toward a life of holiness and devotion to God.

Romans 6 sets forth the argument that Christians should turn away from sin because they have received grace from God. The argument is laid out in four great truths that every Christian should understand and embrace. As you follow the progression of thought in Paul's argument, you will notice that, in a delightful irony, death leads to freedom and life leads to slavery—yet each result is good.

[Please refer to Romans 6 while reading this Pocket Principle™.]

DEAD TO SIN

When Paul writes in Romans 6:2 that Christians have died to sin, he is not stating something that he wishes were true or something that really should be true—he is stating a fact. The problem is not that we haven't died to sin, but rather that we often don't understand what it means.

What "death to sin" does not mean

To be dead to sin does not mean that we have become unresponsive to sin, as some Christians wrongly believe. Those who draw this conclusion do so by misunderstanding Paul's use of the metaphor of death. Because a dead person does not respond to stimuli (such as heat, light, pain, and so on), some believe that the Christian no longer responds to the stimulus of sin. However, three problems immediately surface with this interpretation—it doesn't correspond with our experience, it doesn't correspond with other teachings in Scripture, and it doesn't correspond with the meaning of Christ's death to sin. Wrong thinking on this point leads to denial, deception, despair, and disillusionment—as the Christian is torn between his understanding of Scripture and his personal experience.

> It is true that the closer we draw to God the more aware we become of our sinfulness.

It should be obvious to everyone that a person continues to struggle with sin even after becoming a Christian. In fact, it is the experience of many that the struggle becomes greater, at least for a time. This may be partly because Satan angrily lashes out at the new Christian and sends extraordinary temptations his way, hoping to make him stumble. It is also true that the closer we draw to God, the more aware we become of our sinfulness. What we previously did without thinking, we now know is wrong and struggle to avoid.

The interpretation that we become unresponsive to sin is also inconsistent with Scripture. Christians are instructed to fight against sinful impulses. Paul admonishes us to "not let sin reign in your mortal body" (Romans 6:12) and to "put to death the misdeeds of the body." (Romans 8:13) Paul would not need to direct Christians in these ways if we were unresponsive to sin.

Thirdly, this interpretation does not correspond with the meaning of Christ's death to sin. Paul indicates that, in some way, our death to sin is similar to the death Christ died. However, we know that He did not need to die to become unresponsive to sin. Unlike us, Christ was never responsive (alive) to sin in the first place. Therefore, He didn't need to die to it in the same way we do. The similarity between our death and Christ's has nothing to do with being unresponsive to sin.

What "death to sin" does mean

When writers use an analogy, they typically do so to make one primary point of comparison. So we need to determine what that point of comparison is when Paul uses the analogy of death.

To properly define the phrase "dead to sin" we need to start from Biblical ideas about death rather than from the properties of dead people. In Scripture, death sometimes refers to a death other than physical death. It is often spoken of in moral and legal terms. Spiritual death is referred to as being separated from God, who is the source of all life (Isaiah 59:2).

For example, when Paul wrote to the Ephesians that, prior to salvation, they were dead in their trespasses and sins, he was speaking of spiritual death (Ephesians 2:1). Also, in Romans 5:21, "So just as sin ruled over all people and brought them to death, now God's wonderful grace rules instead, giving us right standing with God and resulting in eternal life through Jesus Christ our Lord." (*NLT*), he again was referring to death as eternal separation from God. Similarly, in Romans 6:23, death refers to spiritual death which, in this context, is a legal consequence of sin. The wages of sin is contrasted to the gift of God, and death is contrasted to eternal life.

Christ's death paid the penalty for sin. This is what Paul means in Romans 6:10 when he says Christ died to sin. Paul also indicates that our death to sin is the same as Christ's death to sin. This means that we, like Christ, are no longer under sin's penalty. Christ paid the penalty; we enjoy freedom from the penalty.

Freedom from the power of sin means that the Christian does not have to sin. He now has a choice.

Now that we've seen what death to sin means, we need to ask how we died to sin. Or, to put it another way, how did Christ's death to sin become our death to sin? In some mysterious way Christians are included in Christ's death. The Christian has been united with Christ in such a way that what is true of Christ is true of the Christian (this is a key positional truth—see Pocket Principle™ #1 in this series). Therefore when Christ died, the Christian, in one sense, also died. It is as if, in the mind of God, when Christ was crucified on the cross, each individual Christian was hanging there with Him.

Our dying with Christ is symbolized by baptism. Paul indicates in Romans 6:3-5 that, when we were baptized in Christ, we were baptized into His death. Baptism symbolizes several things, including cleansing from sin and the anointing of the Holy Spirit, but the primary point of symbolism is union with Christ, which is the basis for our death to sin.

FREE FROM THE SLAVERY OF SIN

We have just seen that, because we are united with Christ in His death, we have been freed from the penalty of sin. However, we have also been freed from the power of sin. This, too, is part of Paul's teaching in Romans 6. He writes that "our old self was crucified…so that the body ruled by sin might be done away with (rendered powerless), that we should no longer be slaves to sin." (Romans 6:6) In Romans 6:18 he states succinctly, "You have been set free from sin."

This teaching does not mean that the Christian will never sin again or be tempted to sin. We have already noted that both experience and Scripture counter this notion. The Christian's battle with sin will continue right up to his death. Freedom from the power of sin means that the Christian does not have to sin. He now has a choice.

Well-known pastor and Bible teacher Charles Swindoll refers to Romans 6 as the Christian's Emancipation Proclamation. In his magnificent work titled *The Grace Awakening*, Swindoll speaks of the tragedy of emancipated slaves who continued in slavery after the Civil War. He notes that "a war had been fought. A president has been assassinated. An amendment to the Constitution has been signed into law. Once-enslaved men, women, and children were now legally emancipated. Yet amazingly, many continued living in fear and squalor. In a context of hard-earned freedom, slaves chose to remain as slaves." Swindoll goes on to speak of the greater tragedy of Christians who continue to live as slaves to sin. "Even though our Great Emancipator, Christ the Lord, paid the ultimate price to overthrow slavery once for all, most Christians act as though they're still held in bondage. In fact, strange as it is, most seem to prefer the security of slavery to the risks of freedom." [1] So we understand that, when Paul asks in Romans 6:2, "We are those who have died to sin; how can we live in it any longer?" he is speaking to the absurdity of, not the impossibility of, continuing in sin. As noted in Swindoll's example, a freed slave can choose to continue to obey his ex-master. It is not impossible, but it is tragic.

[If you have a question about what the terms "old self" or "body of sin" in Romans 6:6 mean, refer to the special note on pg. 59.]

ALIVE TO GOD

Not only have Christians died to sin, they also have become alive to God (Romans 6:11). As noted previously, we all begin our physical lives spiritually dead (Ephesians 2:1). However, at conversion we pass from spiritual death to spiritual life (Romans 6:13). Just as spiritual death means separation from God, spiritual life means relationship with God. Christ has removed the barrier of sin that separated us from God and has made it possible for us to have a relationship with Him. The benefits of new life in Christ are many and include fellowship with Him, help with temptation and struggles, guidance and direction, and His enabling power to live the Christian life.

Sometimes Christians seem to believe that our eternal life begins in heaven. The truth is that it begins the instant we believe and are granted new life in Christ.

Until the Lord returns for His church, every person will experience physical death. However, for the Christian, spiritual (eternal) life has already begun and is not interrupted by physical death.

The difference between spiritual and physical life and death is highlighted in the account of Jesus raising His friend Lazarus from the dead. Lazarus died physically. He was put in a tomb and had been there four days before Jesus arrived in Bethany. Lazarus's sisters Martha and Mary spoke to Jesus and bemoaned the fact that He had not been there to prevent Lazarus from dying. In response, Jesus made this startling proclamation: "I am the resurrection and the life. The one who believes in me will live, even though they die; and whoever lives by believing in me will never die." (John 11:25) Jesus then demonstrated His lordship over life and death by raising Lazarus back to physical life. More importantly, he proclaimed His lordship over spiritual life and death. Although raised from the dead, Lazarus would later return to the grave. However, Lazarus and all others who place their trust in Christ will never die spiritually.

Our new life in Christ is also symbolized by baptism. Just as baptism is a picture of our death with Christ, so also it is a picture of our resurrection with Him. As Paul writes in Romans 6:4-5, "We were therefore buried with Him through baptism into death in order that, just as Christ was raised from the dead through the glory of the Father, we too may live a new life. For if we have been united with Him in a death like His, we will certainly also be united with Him in a resurrection like His." Going down into the water symbolizes death; coming up out of the water symbolizes resurrection and new life.

SLAVES TO RIGHTEOUSNESS

We noted earlier that death to sin leads to freedom from slavery to sin. Now we consider that new life in Christ leads to slavery to God (Romans 6:15-18). This is the natural implication of being alive to God. We now live our lives in Him and for Him. However, this "slavery" is actually gloriously liberating rather than demeaning and defeating as the old slavery to sin was. Slavery to sin is a downward spiral; slavery to righteousness elevates the Christian to an ever-higher position of fellowship with God.

The image of slavery is important. Jesus told the crowds as He was teaching on the mountainside that no person can serve two masters (Matthew 6:24). A person can hold more than one job at a time. Conceivably, someone could even be a servant in one household as a day job and moonlight as a servant in another household in the evenings or on weekends. However, one can only be a slave to

> To submit ourselves to Christ's lordship means that we are making a radical break from sin to follow Christ wholeheartedly.

one master. There is no freedom of allegiance to pursue additional employment or other interests. Servants have a choice of whether or not to continue employment; slaves have no say in the matter.

Just as a person cannot be a part-time spouse, so the Christian cannot be a part-time slave to righteousness. As noted Bible teacher Vance Havner points out, "A wife who is 85% faithful to her husband is not faithful at all. There is no such thing as part-time loyalty to Jesus Christ." [2] To submit ourselves to Christ's lordship means that we are making a radical break from sin to follow Christ wholeheartedly. To continue in habitual sin is an absurd contradiction to our commitment to serve God.

When a Christian commits his life to God at salvation he is, in effect, giving up control of his life. He may not understand the full implications of his decision at the time, but he is turning over the controls to God. The good news is that we can trust God at the controls. We may not always understand where He is leading or what He is doing, but we know the end result is for our good.

CONCLUSION

In the seventh chapter of Luke, we read the account of Jesus having a meal in the house of a Pharisee named Simon. While they were dining, a "woman of the street" came in and worshipped Jesus, washing his feet with perfume and with tears of gratitude for His forgiveness and acceptance. As we might well imagine, this intrusion caused more than a little discomfort among those present at dinner. Jesus knew what His host was thinking and told him a story to illustrate the truth that the one who has been forgiven much, loves much.

This snapshot from the ministry of Christ demonstrates not only the "scandal" of grace but also the natural implications of receiving grace. The scandal is that a prostitute should receive grace just as freely as a Pharisee. The repentant and grateful prostitute walks in freedom and holiness while the self-righteous Pharisee continues in his stubborn slavery to sin, to his own importance, and to the opinions of others.

What glorious freedom we have in Christ Jesus! Freedom from the penalty of sin. Freedom from the power of sin. And one day, in heaven, we shall be free from the presence of sin. When we recognize and embrace these truths, the result will be a life of godly pursuit, not a life of abusing grace by continuing in persistent sin.

*Special Note:

The interpretation of these two phrases, "old self" and "body of sin," is important because how they are defined has a great impact on how people view the Christian growth process. While there is considerable debate about the meaning of these two phrases, the overall conclusion remains the same: we are no longer slaves to sin.

Most likely the "old self" refers to "our old way of life" (Ephesians 4:22) meaning that we were formerly dominated by our sin nature. The "old self" is not a reference to the sin nature for that would mean that the sin nature is dead. Other passages clearly state that the sin nature is still alive in the Christian (Romans 7:18; Galatians 5:17).

The "body of sin" is most likely a reference to the sin nature. If this is correct, then the verb (katargo) that follows cannot mean "done away with." It would be better to translate it "rendered powerless" (as in the NIV footnote) since the sin nature continues to exist.

End Notes:

1. Chuck Swindoll, *The Grace Awakening* (Nashville, Tennessee: Word Publishing, 1990), 105.
2. Source Unknown

7 Grace And Sin

GOAL:

For a disciple to understand his relationship to sin and choose righteousness each day.

GETTING STARTED:

Suppose that as a high school senior you decided to become a doctor. How would this choice affect the rest of your life?

STUDYING TOGETHER:

1. Romans 6:2 says, "We are those who have died to sin." The correct meaning of this phrase may not be obvious. This does not mean that we are unresponsive to sin. What are indicators in your life that you are still responsive to sin?

Read Romans 6:12-13.

2. What does Paul say about being unresponsive to sin?

Read Romans 6:3-5.

3. The key to understanding the phrase "died to sin" is found in Romans 6:3-5.
    What is the relationship between Christ's death and ours?

Read Ephesians 2:1-2.

4. What does Paul mean when he says that we "were dead in [our]
    transgressions and sins"?

5. How is "dead in your transgressions and sins" (Ephesians 2:1) different than
    "died to sin" (Romans 6:2)?

Read Romans 6:11 and Ephesians 2:4-6.

6. What does it mean to be "alive to God"?

Read Romans 6:16-22.

7. Why does Paul use the image of slavery to describe the Christian life?

LOOKING AT REAL LIFE:

8. What are some of the differences in everyday life between having sin as master and having God as Master?

9. What are some of the things that make it difficult for a Christian to submit to God as Lord?

LOOKING AT MY LIFE:

How do you see God's grace operating in your life?

Write a prayer about your appreciation for God and what He has done for you.

Law And Grace

How would you like to go to a school where you could only pass by scoring a perfect 100% on every test or be in a baseball league where you could only play for the team if you got a hit every time you were at bat? It would be difficult, if not impossible, to ace every test. And it would definitely be impossible to get a hit every time at bat. The highest career batting average of any major leaguer belongs to Ty Cobb, who hit .366 over the course of his career. In a hundred years of professional baseball, only 23 players have career batting averages higher than .333, which is only one hit in every three times at bat.

Trying to bat 1.000 is like trying to keep God's law—the standard is perfection. As James reminded his readers, to fail at one point is to break the whole law (James 2:10). This may not seem fair until we remember that God is the author of all moral law so, if you break even one, you have broken the entire law of God. It's like hanging onto a chain over the edge of a precipice. Even if only one link in the chain breaks, you still fall, regardless of the other links that remain unbroken.

Thankfully, as we saw earlier in our study of positional truths, we are not saved by our own efforts. Otherwise, no one would ever make it. As Paul tells us in Romans 3:28, we are saved by faith and not by keeping the law. Furthermore, Paul points out that, as Christians, we are not under the law but under grace (Romans 6:14). This fact raises an important question. What is the Christian's relationship to the law? Is it set aside entirely or does it still have some value or play some role in the life of the Christian?

> Our release from the demands of the law opens a new way of obeying God's commands.

The answer to this question is important, and is one that is often misunderstood. Noted 19th century British preacher and theologian Charles Spurgeon once observed, "There is no point upon which men make greater mistakes than upon the relationship that exists between the Law and the Gospel." [1] The Christian can gain an understanding of her relationship with the law by studying the following key truths taught in Romans 7.

CHRISTIANS HAVE DIED TO THE LAW

A person remains under the law until she dies (Romans 7:1-3). While a person's name might be cleared posthumously, it is rare that a person would be tried for a crime after her death because there would be no point in it. The phrase "death settles all claims" is applicable here. The law no longer has a claim on the Christian because she has died to it.

To illustrate how the law applies to a person only until death, Paul uses the example of marriage. The marriage covenant is in effect (or at least it is supposed to be) as long as both parties to it remain alive. Hence the use of the words in the wedding vows, "Till death us do part." However, when one party dies, the other is no longer bound by the covenant of marriage. In the same way, when we died with Christ, we were freed from the law.

To explain the Christian's relationship to the law, Paul returns to the theme of Christ's death and our union with Him in this event. In the previous chapter (Romans 6), his focus was the Christian's death to sin through Christ. Here, he turns his attention to the Christian's death to the law. We died to the law because death was the penalty the law imposed for failure to keep it. We are free from the curse (penalty) of the law because the demands of the law have been met in the death of Christ. The *NLT* renders Romans 7:4 this way: "So, my dear brothers and sisters, this is the point: You died to the power of the law when you died with Christ. And now you are united with the one who was raised from the dead. As a result, we can produce a harvest of good deeds for God."

> The law…It's like the light that reveals how dirty the room is, not the broom that sweeps it clean.

Our release from the demands of the law opens a new way of obeying God's commands. Quoting the *NLT* again, "But now we have been released from the law, for we died to it and are no longer captive to its power. Now we can serve God, not in the old way of obeying the letter of the law, but in the new way of living in the Spirit." (Romans 7:6) John Stott offers this perspective in his commentary on Romans titled *Men Made New*: "How can I be at the same time both free from the law and obliged to keep it? The paradox is not hard to resolve. We are set free from the Law as a way of acceptance, but obliged to keep it as a way of holiness." [2]

THE NON-CHRISTIAN AND THE LAW

If the Christian is set free from the law through union with Christ and His death, it stands to reason that the non-Christian, who neither knows Christ nor has died with Him, is still under the law.

Non-Christians cannot keep the law.

In their Gospel accounts, Matthew, Mark, and Luke include the story of a man who came to Jesus asking what good things he needed to do to inherit eternal life. Jesus told the man that, if he kept all the commandments, he could have eternal life. Of course Jesus knew that this was impossible, as one would have to be perfect to do so. Jesus' disciples, who were listening in on the conversation, asked, "Who then can be saved?" Christ's reply to them highlights our inability to keep the law. He said, "With man this is impossible, but with God all things are possible." (Matthew 19:26)

In Romans 7:7-13, Paul writes about his relationship to the law as a non-Christian. His experience corresponds to the reality of every non-Christian. He found himself unable to keep the law of God and, in fact, the law only showed him how much of a sinner he was. Worse still, the law actually aroused more sin in Paul.

In some sense, these verses really highlight just how bad or evil sin is. The extreme "sinfulness" of sin is seen when the law (a good thing) causes death (an evil thing). Romans 7:13b says, "So we can see how terrible sin really is. It uses God's good commands for its own evil purposes." (*NLT*) Similarly, education is a good thing, something that most of us want for ourselves and for our children. But education (a good thing) can be exploited and used to teach hate, racism, and immorality (evil purposes). However, the evil intent of those who misuse education does not change the inherent goodness in education.

So Paul notes that the law, which was supposed to bring life, instead brought the penalty of death (Romans 7:10). Inability to keep the law condemns the non-Christian. However, the problem is not with the law; it is with the sinner (with Paul, with you, and with me).

<u>The law is given to bring the non-Christian to Christ.</u>

A number of metaphors have been used to describe the purpose of the law. It's like the dentist's mirror that reveals the cavity, not the drill that repairs it. It's like the plumb line that shows whether something is straight, but it cannot straighten out anything that is crooked. It's like the light that reveals how dirty the room is, not the broom that sweeps it clean.

Another example might help. Consider the situation of a very sick child. The initial tests are inconclusive, but the doctor suspects that the child might have a serious condition. He sends the child to a specialist who uses the latest technology to diagnose her condition. Sure enough, the results confirm the suspected disease. Crushed, the parents try to grasp the implications. But do they blame the doctor or the diagnostic equipment? Of course not. Only now can they try to treat the disease.

Paul writes in Galatians 3:24 that, "the law was our guardian until Christ came." In the original language, the word he uses is that of a trusted slave who leads the master's child to school. The law cannot save us from our sin, but it raises our consciousness of sin (Romans 3:19-20). The law could not save us, but it helped lead us to Christ—the only one who can save.

THE CHRISTIAN AND THE LAW

In the next few verses, Paul switches to the present tense to show his present relationship to the law as a Christian. His thoughts here communicate important truths that apply to all Christians. We note that he affirms the goodness of the law, but also that he still struggles to live according to the law.

Before we go further, it might be helpful to clarify what we mean when we talk about the law. The Old Testament law is often divided into three parts—moral, ceremonial, and civil. The writers of Scripture did not use these terms or necessarily make the same distinctions. However, now that we have the advantage of the full record of God's revelation to people, there is general agreement among most theologians that these categories make sense.

The moral law generally includes the Ten Commandments and the law of love ("Love the LORD your God with all your heart and with all your soul and with all your strength."—first recorded in Deuteronomy 6:5). The moral law represents the character, nature, and will (or purposes) of God and applies to all Christians in all times. The ceremonial and civil laws are also a reflection of God's character; they extend beyond the moral law to give directions on how to relate to God and how to relate to society. Although the principles behind the ceremonial and civil laws are timeless and important to discover and embrace, these laws were given in specific situations for specific purposes. The ceremonial law looks forward to the coming Messiah, while the civil law governed the nation of Israel as a theocracy set apart for God.

The Christian's attitude toward the law

Paul's attitude toward the law provides the example of how every Christian should think of the law. Simply put, Paul affirmed the goodness of the law. In Romans 7:12 he writes that, "the law is holy, and the commandment is holy, righteous, and good." Paul delighted in the law of God (Romans 7:22) and desired to obey its teachings (Romans 7:18).

However, Paul acknowledged that there was something different about the law since the coming of the Messiah. When Paul writes in Romans 10:4 that, "Christ is the end of the law," (*NASB*) he appears to be speaking in terms of fulfillment rather than of termination. He implies that all the requirements of the law have been met in Christ. To those who believe, Christ is now our righteousness.

Paul also acknowledged that all the requirements of the law could be summed up in the "law of love." (Galatians 5:14) In Romans 13:8-10 he writes, "Let no debt remain outstanding, except the continuing debt to love one another, for whoever loves others has fulfilled the law. The commandments, 'You shall not commit adultery,' 'You shall not murder,' 'You shall not steal,' 'You shall not covet,' and whatever other command there may be, are summed up in this one command: 'Love your neighbor as yourself.' Love does no harm to a neighbor. Therefore love is the fulfillment of the law."

<u>Christ's attitude toward the law</u>

In essence, Paul's attitude toward the law reflected the attitude of Christ. Jesus affirmed the goodness of the law and indicated that He had come to fulfill it rather than to break it or to abolish it. Speaking to the crowds on a mountainside, Jesus warned them against breaking the law and then said, "Whoever practices and teaches these commands will be called great in the kingdom of heaven." (Matthew 5:19b)

True righteousness deals with issues of the heart.

The law was a frequent source of dispute between Christ and the religious leaders of His day. They were infuriated that He refused to subject Himself to the man-made additions to the law, and they constantly tried to trip Him up. They often accused Christ of being a lawbreaker. He acknowledged their adherence to man-made regulations, but insisted that wasn't enough. He also taught that it was not enough simply to abstain from outward acts of transgression. True righteousness deals with issues of the heart. In a delicious bit of irony, Jesus, who was accused of not keeping the law, told the crowds, "unless your righteousness surpasses that of the Pharisees and the teachers of the law, you will certainly not enter the kingdom of heaven." (Matthew 5:20)

Jesus, too, taught that love was the fulfillment of the law. One day when Jesus was teaching, an expert in the law asked Him which was the greatest commandment in the law. Jesus replied, "'Love the Lord your God with all your heart and with all your soul and with all your mind.' This is the first and greatest commandment. And the second is like it: 'Love your neighbor as yourself.' All the Law and the Prophets hang on these two commandments." (Matthew 22:37-40)

<u>The Christian's struggle to keep the law</u>

The struggle Paul describes as he seeks to keep God's law again rings true for the Christian. Paul admits that he is unable in his own power to overcome the sin nature (Romans 7:18). He describes himself as not being able to do what he wants, as doing what he hates, and as being a prisoner of the law of sin (verses 19 and 23).

> Positionally, Paul knew that he was no longer a slave to sin; experientially he still struggled to do what was right, just as each of us do.

Paul's plain confession has caused some to debate about whether he is describing his life as a Christian or as a non-Christian. Some would argue that he could not possibly be describing himself as a Christian, because he appears to still be a slave to sin. Yet, he wrote in Romans 6:6 that the Christian is no longer a slave to sin. However, Paul's switch to the present tense seems to indicate that he is talking about his present experience as a Christian. Also, Paul's opinion of the law (and of himself) strongly points to his writing as a mature Christian. He states that he delights in the law and wants to keep it (Romans 7:15-20,22). It seems as though the apparent contradiction comes down to the difference between positional and experiential truth. Positionally, Paul knew that he was no longer a slave to sin; experientially he still struggled to do what was right, just as each of us do.

The fact that Paul does not mention the Holy Spirit in this section is significant and begins to clear up the confusion. It seems to indicate that he is describing himself as a Christian who is trying to follow God and to overcome sin in his own power (without the Holy Spirit). As we shall see in the next Pocket Principle™, it is the empowering presence of the Holy Spirit in our lives that enables us to please God.

CONCLUSION

In Romans chapters 6 and 7, Paul continues his systematic treatment of positional truths. In earlier chapters, he led us to see our desperate need for God for our justification. (See Pocket Principles® #2 & #3 in this series.) Now we see that we just as desperately need God for our sanctification (ongoing growth into Christlikeness). We cannot save ourselves, and we cannot live a life worthy of our calling apart from the gracious intervention and assistance of God in our lives. God sent His Son to provide for our salvation (Romans 8:3), and He sends His Spirit to provide for our continued growth and to enable us to keep His righteous requirements. This will be the subject of the next Pocket Principle™. In the meantime, the words of Philippians 1:6 bring encouragement: "He who began a good work in you will carry it on to completion until the day of Christ Jesus."

End Notes:

1. Rev. C.H. Spurgeon, *Law and Grace*, sermon delivered on Sabbath morning, August 26, 1855, at New Park Street Chapel, Southwark (Source: www.spurgeon.org/sermons/0037.php).

2. John Stott, *Men Made New* (Grand Rapids, Michigan: Baker Book House, 1966), 82.

Law And Grace

8

GOAL:

For a disciple to understand the role of the law in a Christian's life.

GETTING STARTED:

Imagine that you attend a school in which you must score 100% to pass a test. How would you feel about that and how might you react?

STUDYING TOGETHER:

Read Romans 3:19-20.

1. According to this passage, what is a non-Christian's relationship to the law?

The law can point out sin, but it cannot cure it. The non-Christian can only gain salvation through faith in Christ, not by keeping the law.

2. Does this mean that the law has no significance to the Christian? Why or why not?

Read Romans 7:1-3.

3. Summarize Paul's main point in this passage.

Read Romans 7:4.

4. What does Paul mean when he says that Christians have "died to the law through the body of Christ"?

5. According to this verse, what are two of the benefits of dying to the law for Christians?

Read Romans 7:6.

6. According to this verse, what is the change a Christian will experience by dying to the law?

Read Romans 8:3b-4.

7. According to these verses, what does the Holy Spirit enable the Christian to do?

8. Looking back at all the verses in questions 1-7, what is the Christian's new relationship to the law?

Read Romans 7:15-20.

9. What problem does Paul imply here with regards to Christians who are trying to keep the law?

LOOKING AT REAL LIFE:

10. If a Christian does not correctly understand her relationship to the law, what effects will this have on her relationship with God?

LOOKING AT MY LIFE:

As you have worked your way through this study, how has it challenged or changed your view of the relationship of the law to the Christian life?

9 Walking In The Power Of The Holy Spirit

In the previous Pocket Principle™, we focused on the impossibility of the Christian living a life pleasing to God in his own power. However, if God wants us to live holy lives (and Scripture clearly indicates this is so), then He must have made a way for this to be possible. What makes it possible is that the true Christian is indwelled by the Holy Spirit (Romans 8:9). It is His presence in our lives that gives us power to live holy lives that are pleasing to God (Romans 8:4).

We live in the Information Age—one where technology is increasingly important, not only in the marketplace but in almost every area of our lives. The younger generation is embracing and learning to use computers as easily as most of us learned to ride a bicycle. However, some adults have had challenges adapting to new technology. Most of us have heard about "dumb things" people say when they call for assistance with their computers. There's the story of the lady who put her computer mouse on the floor and tried to use it like a sewing machine pedal. Another person thought he could add space to his hard drive by creating new directories. Less believable is the lady who thought she could scan a document by pressing it against her computer monitor. Perhaps the "dumbest" thing is when people call for help only to realize they have not even connected their computers to the power source.

> It is His presence in our lives that gives us power to live holy lives that are pleasing to God.

Sadly, some Christians try to live this way. They profess to want to follow Christ and walk in obedience to His commands, yet they continue in old patterns of behavior. Or, to borrow Paul's language, they continue to walk according to the flesh rather than according to the Spirit. They do not take advantage of the Spirit's power in their lives.

Romans 8:11 tells us that the indwelling presence of the Holy Spirit is a guarantee of our eventual resurrection. We will be raised with glorified bodies—perfectly holy (Philippians 3:21). So, by the Spirit's power, we are already becoming what we will one day fully become. The Spirit's presence in our lives provides a reminder that holiness is in line with our final outcome.

It is interesting to note that the Holy Spirit is mentioned only twice in the three previous chapters of Romans. It is almost as though Paul wanted his readers to share his sense of frustration and impotence in trying to overcome sin and please God without the empowering of the Holy Spirit. He wanted them to fully comprehend their inability to live the Christian life on their own. But here, in chapter eight, Paul focuses intently on the ministry of the Spirit in our lives. In fact, the Spirit is mentioned more in the eighth chapter of Romans than in any other chapter in the entire Bible.

In Romans 8:4, Paul introduces the idea of living according to the Spirit. Then, in the following verses, he develops the idea of how to do this. Because the Holy Spirit lives in all Christians, He makes it possible for them to walk by the Spirit. If they do this, they will not carry out the desires of the sin nature, but instead, they will live according to God's law.

Sometimes when Paul uses the word "if" it is to emphasize the "trueness" of a statement; sometimes it is to emphasize that the statement is conditional. In Romans 8:9, he writes, "If indeed the Spirit of God lives in you," and the implication is that He does. In verse ten, he writes, "But if Christ is in you," and the implication is that He is. However, Paul uses "if" in the conditional sense when he writes in verse 13 of Roman 8, "If by the Spirit you put to death the misdeeds of the body, you will live." Paul does not assume that the reader is walking according to the Spirit. He only says that if this is true, then the result will be true. Walking by the Spirit is not automatic, and it is not passive. However, Christians can walk by the Spirit by applying the truths taught in Romans 8:5-8,12-13.

SETTING OUR MINDS ON THE DESIRES OF THE SPIRIT (ROMANS 8:4-5)

The importance of the mind

Paul contrasts the spiritual self and the fleshly self. There are two different conditions that lead to two different ways of thinking, that lead to two different ways of acting, that lead to two different results. Those who live according to the flesh think about fleshly things and engage in sinful desires that end in death. Those who live according to the Spirit think about things that please Him and engage in righteous behaviors that end in life and peace (Romans 8:6).

All people have indwelling sin; only the Christian has the indwelling Spirit.

The key is our mindset. Our ability to live according to the Spirit and thus to fulfill the righteous requirements of the law is greatly dependent on our mental focus. It helps distinguish whether we live according to the Spirit or not. That is why Paul writes in Romans 12:2 that our behavior is transformed by the renewing of our minds.

We think about the things that are important to us. These are the background tapes that are constantly playing in our minds. A good test of the focus of our mind is to ask where it goes when it has a chance. Where does your mind rest when it's at rest? Or, to put it another way, when your mind is in neutral, into which gear does it most easily slip? The question is not what you think about when carving a turkey, or when threading a needle, or when pulling out into heavy traffic. Then you are concentrating on the task at hand. No, the question is what you think about when relaxing after a turkey dinner or when driving along in steady traffic.

I (Jon) greatly enjoy gardening, and I like to build things. I'm presently combining both passions by dreaming up ideas for a garden shed I plan to build. My mind keeps going back to the plans, whether at work, driving in traffic, or lying in bed trying to get to sleep. I have to admit that, as I sit at the computer typing, a couple of times I have wondered again whether the window should go on the back or on one of the sides of the shed. Thankfully, while my desires in this example are not overtly spiritual, they are not sinful. I wish this were always the case.

<u>The importance of choice</u>

All people have indwelling sin; only the Christian has the indwelling Spirit. The non-Christian has a sin nature but does not have the Holy Spirit. Therefore he habitually chooses to live according to the sin nature (Romans 7:7-8). The result is a mind set on the flesh, which leads to death (Romans 5:6). This mindset reinforces the non-Christian's hostility toward God, and destroys relationships with others, and with himself.

Because the Christian still has a sin nature and now has the Holy Spirit, he has a choice where he will set his mind. He can set his mind either on the desires of the Spirit or on the desires of the flesh. The result of his choice will have consequences. Setting his mind on the flesh damages his relationship with God and with others, and negatively impacts his own sense of wholeness and health. However, the mind set on the Spirit is life and peace. This person is alive to God, alert to spiritual realities, and thirsty for righteousness. He experiences harmony with God, with others, and with himself.

A Spirit-directed mindset enables us to do the will of God. In his first letter to the Christians at Corinth, Paul writes that the Spirit knows the mind of God. Through the Spirit we can have "the mind of Christ" if we choose to set our mind on the desires of the Spirit (I Corinthians 2:10b-16). The words of an old Christian hymn become true in our lives—"May the mind of Christ my Savior live in me from day to day."

Our mindset is dependent on two things—not just the presence of the Holy Spirit but also what we choose to think about. The presence of the Holy Spirit is necessary to a renewed mind, but it is not sufficient. It provides the opportunity but does not guarantee the certainty. For example, for a car to provide transportation it needs certain parts such as an engine and a steering wheel. Having all the right parts is necessary, but it is not sufficient. The car also needs fuel and a driver if it is to actually go anywhere. Having the Holy Spirit living in us is not sufficient for growth in godliness; we must choose to set our minds on the things of the Spirit.

In Philippians 4:8, Paul instructs the Christians at Philippi that they should choose to focus on the right things—-things that are true, noble, right, pure, lovely, admirable, excellent, and praiseworthy. A good way to do this is to meditate on God's Word (see Psalms 1 and 119).

PUTTING TO DEATH THE MISDEEDS OF THE BODY BY THE SPIRIT

Paul writes in Romans 8:12 that the Christian has no obligation whatsoever to the sinful nature to continue to follow its destructive desires. What is implied is that the Christian does have an obligation to God: to walk according to the Spirit. The indwelling presence of the Holy Spirit is God's gift to the Christian. Walking with the Spirit is the Christian's gift to God.

Part of what it means to walk according to the Spirit is to put to death the acts of the flesh. This matter of putting to death the misdeeds of the body by the Spirit is often called mortification. From the same root word, we get words like "mortician" and "mortuary." Describing a wonderful paradox, Paul writes in Romans 8:13 that there is a kind of life lived according to the sin nature that leads to death and a kind of death (mortification) that leads to life. Mortification is a clear-sighted recognition of the evil that is in us combined with a radical commitment to put it to death.

We must choose to set our minds on things of the Spirit.

Paul doesn't get specific about the details here—he just says to do it. What that looks like practically may vary from person to person and perhaps, from sin to sin. There are different ways to "kill" a sin just as there are different ways to kill a plant. I can put a plant to death through neglect, through starvation, through cutting it off, through uprooting it, through poisoning, and so on. Many sins may need to be starved to death—if you don't feed them, they will die. Other sins may need to be uprooted, cut off, or whatever else works.

The important thing is that the sin is dealt with severely and effectively. Mortification is not passive. We have to take the initiative and aggressively deal with areas of sin in our lives. The problem for most of us isn't that we don't know the most effective way to put a sinful habit to death—the problem is we're not serious enough about it.

That we should take sin seriously is highlighted by the severity of Christ's words on several occasions (Matthew 18:8-9; Mark 9:43). He said that if your eye causes you to sin, you should pluck it out. If your hand causes you to sin, you should cut it off. Obviously, Jesus is using hyperbole, but He does it to make a point. Holiness before God is so important that we should do whatever it takes to please Him.

The role of the Holy Spirit

It is important to remember that the Christian has a Helper in this matter—a co-executioner, if you will. He can only put to death the misdeeds of the body as he depends on the power and direction of the Holy Spirit. This co-laboring partnership is illustrated in the life of Paul when he writes, "To this end I strenuously contend with all the energy Christ so powerfully works in me." (Colossians 1:29)

The role of the Body of Christ

As Hebrews 10:24-25 reminds us, the Christian also needs words of admonition and support from other Christians. Warning others of sin and encouraging them to stay on paths of righteousness is not just the job of the preacher or Sunday school teacher. Rather, each of us should recognize the obligation we have to one another in this matter. Incidentally, a very strong instrument useful for putting a habit to death is confession and accountability. Jesus' brother James knew the power of this when he wrote, "Confess your sins to each other and pray for each other so that you may be healed." (James 5:16)

CONCLUSION

In the closing verses of Romans 7, Paul writes, "What a wretched man I am! Who will rescue me from this body that is subject to death? Thanks be to God, who delivers me through Jesus Christ our Lord!" (Romans 7:24-25) Paul was already looking forward to Romans chapter 8, where he would explain how we can have consistent victory over sin. The secret is walking according to God's Holy Spirit living in us. This kind of life is possible, but there are two necessary requirements and two necessary actions. The two requirements are our effort and our dependence on the Spirit. The two actions are setting our minds on the desires of the Spirit and putting to death the misdeeds of the body by the Spirit. In this case two plus two equals "for." By doing these things, we can live "for" God.

Walking By The Power Of The Holy Spirit

9

GOAL:

For a disciple to understand the Spirit-directed life and to understand and practice his part in the process.

GETTING STARTED:

What are some situations in which you cannot achieve the desired results without the use of something beyond yourself?

STUDYING TOGETHER:

Read Romans 8:9.

1. In this verse, what is the relationship between the Holy Spirit and the Christian?

Read Galatians 5:16,19-23.

2. According to what Paul says about the sin nature and the Spirit, what is the impact of walking in the Spirit?

3. What evidence do you see of the acts of the sin nature and the fruit of the Spirit expressed in this world?

Read Galatians 5:25.

4. What do you think you need to do to "keep in step with the Spirit"?

Romans 8 suggests two important ways of keeping in step with the Spirit. In verse 5 we find one of the ways Paul suggests to do this.

Read Romans 8:5.

5. According to this verse, what can we do to keep in step with the Spirit?

Read Romans 8:6-8

6. According to these verses, why is it important to keep our minds set on what the Spirit desires?

7. What do you think it means to set your mind on the desires of the Spirit?

Read Psalm 1:1-3 and Philippians 4:8.

8. What do these verses tell us about setting our minds on the desires of the Spirit?

Romans 8 goes on to suggest another important way of keeping in step with the Spirit.

Read Romans 8:13.

9. What are the misdeeds of the body? And what does it means to put them to death?

10. Identify a sin area in your life that causes repeated problems for you. What might it look like in your life if you were to make a serious attempt to "put it to death"?

LOOKING AT REAL LIFE:

11. What are some of the reasons that Christians don't depend on the Holy Spirit more?

LOOKING AT MY LIFE:

What is a major motivation in your life encouraging you to depend on the Spirit?

Grace And Security In Christ

We live in an age of uncertainty. If the stock market volatility, the growing threat of terrorism, and the emergence of new diseases like SARS have taught us anything, it is that we cannot predict what might happen next. Closer to home, company layoffs and broken marriages add to the challenges that rear their ugly heads. Many people are deeply insecure because of the personal hurts and disappointments they have received while living in our chaotic and unpredictable world. Yet we all long for security—to know that there is something, even if just one thing, that we can absolutely count on.

The May 26, 1994 edition of *Bits and Pieces* included the following anecdote: A manager and a sales rep stood looking at a map on which colored pins indicated the company representative in each area. "I'm not going to fire you, Wilson," the manager said, "but I'm loosening your pin a bit just to emphasize the insecurity of your situation." While this conversation could conceivably take place in the business world, the Christian never has to worry that God is in the pin-loosening business. Rather, everything He says to the true Christian reinforces the security and strength of our relationship with Him.

One of the major themes of Romans chapter 8 is the Christian's security in Christ. Paul begins this chapter with a bold statement of "no condemnation" and ends it with a firm conclusion of "no separation." In between, he states several convictions that show the certainty of our salvation and the steadfastness of Christ's love. It is as though he is carefully weaving together multiple threads in the Christian's security blanket.

Christians can have confidence in the security of their relationship with Christ because of the grace received as a result of the work of God in Christ. This truth will be seen as we consider five rhetorical questions posed by Paul in the closing verses of Romans 8.

IF GOD IS FOR US, WHO CAN BE AGAINST US?

The first question can be found in verse 31 where Paul asks, "If God is for us, who can be against us?" The first part of the question is important. Without it, one could think of many who would be against us, including enemies, competitors, the Devil and his angels, and so on. Certainly the Christians in Rome to whom Paul was writing could think of many who might be against them. But, because God is for us, the answer is that no one can prevail against God. Others might come against us, but they will not be successful. That God is for us can be seen in many ways, including the following two ideas that Paul touches on in Romans 8.

God brings good results out of bad experiences for the Christian.

Romans 8:28 is one of the greatest promises made in Scripture to the Christian. It reads as follows: "And we know that in all things God works for the good of those who love Him, who have been called according to His purpose." The promise is made to Christians—to those who have been called by God and have responded to His offer of salvation. Such people have a new perspective—a new mindset that values the eternal over the temporal. This perspective is important when considering the truth of this verse.

This verse is very popular among Christians and for good reason. It brings hope in the midst of hopeless circumstances. Yet, it can be too easy to interpret the promise along the lines of, "Keep your chin up. Things are going to get better." The point is actually much stronger than that—regardless of the circumstances (which may, in fact, be very bad and may get worse) God is going to accomplish His purposes in your life. And His purposes are always good.

Surely the "all things" of verse 28 includes the "sufferings" of verse 17 and the "groanings" of verse 23. This verse does not deny or lessen the reality of evil, pain, and misfortune. Rather, it affirms them within the context of God's greater purposes. All that is negative in this life is seen to have a positive purpose in the execution of God's eternal plan. Life is not the random mess that it sometimes appears to be. One of the most freeing concepts to understand is this—There is nothing I can do, or someone else can do to me, that cannot be redeemed by God for my good and His glory.

Everything God says to the true Christian reinforces the security and strength of her relationship with Him.

Two illustrations of this principle come readily to mind. One of the strongest examples of God's sovereignty and His grace in all of Scripture is the story of Joseph. Joseph faced more hardships and abuse than any of us will ever know. His own brothers mistreated him and sold him into slavery. His master's wife falsely accused him of sexual misconduct and had him thrown into prison. A high-ranking fellow prisoner forgot his promises to Joseph. However, God allowed all this to happen to have His man in the right place at the right time to save the lives of many people. Joseph's perspective, demonstrated in what he said to his brothers was, "You intended to harm me, but God intended it all for good." (Genesis 50:20, *NLT*)

Another verse popular among Christians is Jeremiah 29:11 which reads, "'For I know the plans I have for you,' declares the Lord, 'plans to prosper you and not to harm you, plans to give you hope and a future.'" This grand statement of affirmation and encouragement appears in many places, including calendars, coffee mugs, wall plaques, and T-shirts. What many people may not realize is that these words from God were spoken by the prophet Jeremiah to the nation of Judah as she was going into captivity because of her disobedience to God. Yes, God was going to accomplish His purposes through this situation, but it didn't remove the painful discipline that had to come first.

<u>God completes His work in the Christian.</u>

A second affirmation that God is indeed for us is that He brings His purposes to completion. As we have seen, Paul mentions God's purpose in verse 28. In verses 29 and 30, He explains what that purpose is for each Christian. Paul traces God's good and saving purpose through five stages from its beginning in His mind to its consummation in the coming glory. The stages are God's foreknowledge, predestination, calling, justification and glorification.

Many people have noted that sanctification is omitted from this list and suggest that it is because it is the one aspect that is dependent on our cooperation. While we cannot be certain of Paul's reason for not including sanctification, it is true that each of the other items in his list is an action that God takes on our behalf. Our "contribution" is only to respond in faith as He graciously draws us to Himself.

God's ultimate purpose is to conform us to be like Christ, which will be completed when we are glorified (Romans 8:29). Paul is so confident that God will bring to completion all that He has purposed that he uses a technique termed "the prophetic past" and speaks of our future glorification as though it has already happened (Romans 8:30). In the meantime, the process of sanctification (becoming like Christ) is a foretaste of glorification—when we shall be like Him, for we shall see Him as He is (I John 3:2).

> God's ultimate purpose is to conform us to be like Christ, which will be completed when we are glorified.

It is said of Michelangelo, the famous 16th century Italian artist and sculptor, that he created his masterpieces by seeing the finished product in his mind and then chipping away from the marble everything that didn't look like that product. Little by little, the sculpture would reveal the picture that was in Michelangelo's mind. God already knows what the finished product for each of us looks like, and He is committed to chipping away and ultimately gracing us with His full glory.

WILL HE NOT ALSO GIVE US ALL THINGS?

Paul's next question, found in verse 32, implies that since God gave us His Son (the most He could do), He will also give us everything else that we need. The cross is the guarantee of God's continuing, unfailing generosity. A great example of this generosity can be found in Romans 8. Verse 16 tells us, "The Spirit Himself testifies with our spirit that we are God's children." By the Spirit, we call God "Abba, Father." As children, we are heirs of God and co-heirs with Christ. It is hard for us to even begin to comprehend what this means. This is why, in his letter to the Ephesians, Paul speaks of the "incomparable riches of His grace" (Ephesians 2:7) and the "boundless riches of Christ." (Ephesians 3:8)

Watchman Nee, who was one of the most well known Chinese Christians of the 20th century, tells about a new convert who came in great distress because he was afraid he was losing his salvation. Nee nodded to his dog laying on the floor and pointed out all of his good features—house trained, clean, and obedient. He then said he had an infant son in the other room who throws his food around, fouls his clothes and, in general, creates a mess everywhere he goes. Nee then said to his visitor, "But who is going to inherit my kingdom? Not my dog; my son is my heir. You are Jesus Christ's heir because it is for you that He died." [1] Despite our continued messes, our sure inheritance in Christ brings us great security.

The same Spirit whom Paul refers to in Romans 8:23 as the "firstfruit" of our future glory (the proof of what is yet to come) is also a help to us in our current trouble. He helps us pray and intercedes on our behalf (Romans 8:27). The wonderful gift of the Holy Spirit is a further sign of God's generosity.

WHO WILL BRING ANY CHARGE AGAINST THOSE WHOM GOD HAS CHOSEN?

Paul's point with this rhetorical question in verse 33 is not the impossibility of someone bringing a charge, but the utter futility of it. It is pointless for anyone to bring a charge (although Satan constantly tries to do so), because God has already declared us righteous. When God looks at us, He sees the righteousness of Jesus Christ. We don't have to worry about anyone digging up some dirt on us; our sins have already been washed white as snow.

WHO IS THE ONE WHO CONDEMNS?

This question takes us back to the opening verse of chapter 8 where Paul boldly proclaims, "Therefore, there is now no condemnation for those who are in Christ Jesus." Paul's use of the word "therefore" indicates that he is drawing a conclusion from what has already been said. In this case, he is not referring just to the last thing he said or even to the last chapter he wrote, but to everything he had written thus far. In particular, he is referring to his earlier development of the doctrine of justification by faith. Because we are justified and united with Christ (placed in Christ), we are no longer under condemnation.

With this question in verse 34, Paul implies that Jesus does not condemn us. He died for our sins and rose from the dead for our justification. Now He sits at the Father's right hand interceding on our behalf. The only one who could possibly bring a charge or condemn is actually our advocate.

WHO SHALL SEPARATE US FROM THE LOVE OF CHRIST?

Paul's fifth question highlights the fact that Christians can never be separated from the love of Christ. He is building toward the climax of his argument—the culmination of several chapters—and he deals with this question at length.

In verse 35, he lists seven things that might lead us to think that we have been separated from the love of Christ—trouble, calamity, persecution, hunger, cold, danger, or the threat of death. Then in verse 36, he quotes from Psalms 44:22 to indicate that these types of problems and even persecutions have been the normal experience for God's people throughout history.

> Christians will be the most secure people in the world when they fully grasp what Christ accomplished for them.

In his second letter to the Corinthians (believed to have been written shortly before the book of Romans), Paul describes how he himself had faced all these types of difficulties (II Corinthians 11:23-28). The writer of the book of Hebrews details a similar list as he describes the tribulations of saints down through the ages (Hebrews 11:35b-39). Christ Himself suffered all of these things, and more. He proved His love for us through His sufferings, so it would be ridiculous to think that our sufferings could possibly separate us from His love. Rather, our sufferings should be seen as evidence of our union with Christ (Romans 8:17), not as a cause for doubting His love. In verse 37, Paul proclaims that we are more than conquerors ("hyper conquerors" in the original language) over these things through the love Christ has for us.

In verses 38 and 39, Paul goes on to present one last list of things that might possibly be able to separate us from Christ's love. He speaks of life and death, and the powers of heaven and of hell. Of any aspect of time or space. He rejects them all and ends with "nor anything else in all creation." It is as though he was saying to his reader, "You fill in the blank. It still won't matter." Once a person has become a Christian there is nothing at all, including the actions of the person herself, that can separate her from the love of Christ. She is eternally secure in Christ's love.

CONCLUSION

Many of us have grown up with a performance-based acceptance mentality. Whether it was parents who only showed love when we did what they wanted or friends who only accepted us when we looked a certain way, we learned that many people judge us based on how we act. The result is insecurity. Thankfully, the Christian life is provision-based acceptance rather than performance-based acceptance. The key is—on what basis have we received all these blessings? Christians will be the most secure people in the world when they fully grasp what Christ accomplished for them.

End Note:

1. Watchman Nee, *Our Daily Bread* (Sermon Illustration).

10 Grace And Security In Christ

GOAL:

For a disciple to investigate the reasons she, as a Christian, can have confidence in her security in Christ and grow in that personal security.

GETTING STARTED:

Suppose you are in danger of losing your job. How would that affect your job performance and your mental and emotional outlooks?

STUDYING TOGETHER:

Read Romans 8:28-29.

1. According to verse 29 what is God's ultimate goal for Christians?

2. How does Romans 8:28 fit into that process?

3. How have you seen God work in Christians' lives to develop Christlikeness?

Read Jeremiah 29:10-14.

4. Jeremiah was writing to the Jews who had been exiled to Babylon and held in captivity. What was God's desire for His people?

Read Romans 8:1.

5. What are the benefits to a Christian if she really understands the implications of this verse (there is no condemnation)?

6. What are the consequences to a Christian if she feels that she is under condemnation by God?

Read Romans 8:31-34.

7. Paul further argues that Christians are not under condemnation through a series of rhetorical questions. Explain the arguments Paul is making in each of these questions.

    "If God is for us, who can be against us?"

    "He who did not spare His own son, but gave Him up for us all—how will He not also, along with Him, graciously give us all things?"

    "Who will bring any charge against those whom God has chosen?"

    "Who then is the one who condemns?"

Read Romans 8:35-39.

8. The next question Paul asks is "Who shall separate us from the love of Christ?" Paul lists things that in some people's minds may cause Christians to be separated from God (vs. 38,39) or give evidence of separation (vs. 35b). How does Paul rebut this way of thinking?

LOOKING AT REAL LIFE:

9. Paul says that we are no longer condemned for our sin. He also says we can never be separated from the love of God. Why is it important for the Christian to understand both concepts?

LOOKING AT MY LIFE:

As you review this lesson, what was the most important idea/truth to you personally and why?

Spend some time in the group praising and thanking God for His attributes described in these verses.

What's Next?

We hope you enjoyed this study.
You may be wondering: "So, what's next?"
I'm glad you asked.

If your group has benefited from their experience with this study, we suggest that you continue with the Equipping For Ministry (Phase III) series. The suggested order to study this series is *Spiritual Warfare-I, Evangelism Training Manual* or *Workbook, Positional Truth, Healthy Relationships, Ministry Principles-I,* and *Inductive Bible Study Manual* or *Workbook.* Our *Bible Readings* for Phase III can be used alongside any or all of these resources. An explanation of why we suggest this order can be found on our website. However, you can use our materials in whatever way works best for you and your ministry. (See link on next page.)

Also, **on the WDA website you will find explanations about the meaning of the different Phases I through V.** If you want to understand more about progressive growth there is a free download on our website called *Disciple Building: A Biblical Framework.* This explains the biblical basis for our disciple building process. (See links on next page.)

If you want to understand more about WDA's Restoring Your Heart ministry, there is a free download entitled *How Emotional Problems Develop* on our website. Restoring Your Heart addresses relational and emotional needs that affect a disciple's ability to grow spiritually. (See links on next page.)

We look forward to a long association with you as you seek and follow our Lord, and grow in Christ using WDA Materials.

Bob Dukes

LINKS:

Phase III: Equipping for Ministry:
www.disciplebuilding.org/product-category/equipping-for-ministry-phase-3/

Meaning of Phases I-V:
www.disciplebuilding.org/about/phases-of-christian-growth/2/

Free Download of *Disciple Building: A Biblical Framework*:
www.disciplebuilding.org/store/leadership-manuals/
disciple-building-a-biblical-framework/

Free Download of *How Emotional Problems Develop*:
www.disciplebuilding.org/store/leadership-manuals/
how-emotional-problems-develop/

About Restoring Your Heart:
www.disciplebuilding.org/ministries/restoringyourheart/

About WDA

WDA's mission is to serve the church worldwide by developing Christlike character in people and equipping them to disciple others according to the pattern Jesus used to train His disciples.

Organized as Worldwide Discipleship Association (WDA) in 1974, we are based in the United States and have ministries and partners throughout the world. WDA is a 501c(3) non-profit organization funded primarily by the tax-deductible gifts of those who share our commitment to biblical disciple building.

WDA is committed to intentional, progressive discipleship. We offer a flexible, transferable approach that is based on the ministry and methods of Jesus, the Master Disciple Builder. By studying Jesus' ministry, WDA discovered five phases of Christian growth. The Cornerstone series focuses on the first and second phases, Phase I: Establishing Faith and Phase II: Laying Foundations. Cornerstone addresses the needs of a young Christian or a more mature Christian who wants a review of foundational Christian truths. The Equipping For Ministry phase (Phase III) is geared toward disciples who are ready to learn how to minister to others. The remaining phases are: Phase IV: Developing New Leaders and Phase V: Developing Mature Leaders.

For more information about WDA please visit our website: www.disciplebuilding.org.

If you are interested in seeing other WDA materials, please visit the WDA store: www.disciplebuilding.org/store.

Learn more about Disciple Building at www.disciplebuilding.org.

The following materials are available at the WDA store.
www.disciplebuilding.org/store

Maturity Matters®
Read *Maturity Matters®* by Bob Dukes.

Leaders must understand, balance, and apply the dynamics that contribute to progressive growth and sanctification. This requires both a strong faith and a new focus. As we fix our eyes on things unseen, the outcome will be a deeper faith, drawn in part from church leaders who consistently equip Christians. As we help them put truth into practice, faith grows. The rewards are both temporal and eternal.

Disciple Building: A Biblical Framework
Read *A Biblical Framework* by Bob Dukes.

This book presents the philosophical overview of the discipleship ministry of Christ and how its principles can be applied to disciple building today.

Cornerstone
Begin to build disciples using Cornerstone.

WDA Cornerstone features 38 Bible lessons and essays that help new Christians grow to maturity. These lessons cover the first two phases of growth, Establishing Faith and Laying Foundations. The Cornerstone curriculum is designed to run for approximately one year. Once established, it runs continuously with various entry points. Ideally, it works in concert with Life Coaches, who meet with and help orient disciples to the Christian life and the church community, facilitating and supplementing their involvement in a Discipleship Community.

Life Coaching
Learn how to be a Life Coach.

Life Coaches are Christian leaders who are willing to invest their knowledge and experience and even their very lives so that others might learn to think, feel and act like Jesus. A spiritual Life Coach is a person who, in the midst of a caring relationship, imparts truth that changes the life (conduct/character) of another, gradually helping the disciple become more like Jesus Christ. At WDA, we often use the phrase, "meeting people where they are, helping them take the next step®" to describe the Life Coaching process. Life Coach training offers a philosophical and practical approach that is carried out through the design and implementation of growth projects tailored to individual needs and levels of maturity.

WDA is able to provide Life Coach training in three distinct ways: individual self-study using our *Disciple Building: Life Coaching* manual, group study and interaction at a Life Coaching Seminar or through a 28/20® church ministry consulting relationship. To learn more about Life Coaching go to
www.disciplebuilding.org/ministries/church-ministry/life-coaching.

Watch the Life Coaching Introductory Video: vimeo.com/135056845

Restoring Your Heart
Read *How Emotional Problems Develop.*

Through our experiences discipling people over the years, we at WDA have discovered that unresolved relational and emotional issues from the past can be a stumbling block to spiritual growth.

Our Restorative Ministry trains people in churches and in other ministries to help people through a healing process that will enable them to become healthier in all their relationships, including their relationship with God.

Check out **Restoring Your Heart** at www.disciplebuilding.org/ministries/restorative-ministry.

WDA Partnerships

Help us build disciples worldwide.

You can help us fulfill the great commission by becoming a Worldwide Discipleship Association (WDA) partner. WDA's mission is to serve the church worldwide by developing Christlike character in people and equipping them to disciple others according to the pattern Jesus used to train His disciples.

Since our inception in 1974 our materials and processes have been used in more than 90 U.S. cities and in over **55 countries**. We have created **over a million direct discipleship impacts** and have conducted face-to-face **training to over 17,000 pastors and leaders** around the globe! **Your support of WDA is vital to the success of our mission.** We pledge to serve as faithful stewards of your generous gifts to the ministry.

www.disciplebuilding.org/give/wda-partnership

Become a Partner Today

Made in the USA
Columbia, SC
06 July 2024

38174003R00057